The Revd Canon Andrew Clitherov
ing for the Diocese of Blackburn, ɪ̣ ̣ ̣ ̣ ̣ ̣ ̣ ̣
Cuthbert's Church and St John's Church in Lytham, an Honorary
Canon of Blackburn Cathedral and Chaplain to the Queen. He is
the author of *Into Your Hands: Prayer, and the Call to Holiness in
Everyday Ministry and Life* (2001), *Renewing Faith in Ordained
Ministry: New Hope for Tired Clergy* (2004) and *Creative Love in
Tough Times* (2007), all published by SPCK.

# DESIRE, LOVE
# AND THE RULE
# OF ST BENEDICT

# DESIRE, LOVE AND THE RULE OF ST BENEDICT

Andrew Clitherow

First published in Great Britain in 2008

Society for Promoting Christian Knowledge
36 Causton Street
London SW1P 4ST

*British Library Cataloguing-in-Publication Data*
A catalogue record for this book is available from the British Library

ISBN 978–0–281–05998–0

1 3 5 7 9 10 8 6 4 2

Typeset by Graphicraft Ltd, Hong Kong
Printed in Great Britain by Ashford Colour Press

Produced on paper from sustainable forests

*For Joan and Mike*
*Without their understanding and support,*
*the writing of this book would have*
*taken much longer*

# Contents

# Acknowledgements

Special thanks to my wife Rebekah, for her love and devotion, and to my children Simon, Kate, Emily and Edward, for making my life so special.

Thanks also to the Revd Dr Saskia Barnden for her hard work and thoughtful suggestions and to Alison Barr at SPCK for her encouragement and support.

Thanks also to the people of St Cuthbert's and St John's Lytham and the wider community of the town for their faith and generous spirit.

# Introduction

## Aim

I lament the lack of alternative lifestyle offered by the Church today. I fear that when the historians of the future reflect on the nature of mainstream Christianity in our generation, they will wonder why at a time both of great materialism and soul searching, the Church did not offer a radically different way of life. Sadly, the way the Church conducts its business, and even at times its worship, is pretty much like that of any other organization. Insiders become immune to the nonsense we make of the gospel and outsiders won't waste their time on anything that purports to be radically different and clearly isn't.

Being a Christian is supposed to make a difference to what one believes about oneself and therefore to how one lives. But anyone who has tried to lead this kind of life knows that it is neither simple nor straightforward. Our desires for security and success seem to conflict with our longing for love. But only complete commitment to Christ will unlock for us the secrets of his kingdom. This is the commitment of sacrificial love and service where power politics have no place. We are sometimes afraid to go this far because many who appear to become completely committed, also commit terrible crimes against others in what is essentially their pursuit of power. While extremism is understood today to be the preserve of godless fundamentalists – and there remain plenty of these in the Church as well as in other religious institutions – we can nevertheless be radical in our response to the gospel of Jesus Christ without losing our sanity. This book, therefore, is an attempt to explore a truer understanding of radical love and to suggest how we might live in the light of such love.

Such an approach to faith can be unattractive because for some of the time at least, faith can make life more rather than less complicated. For faith is not so much about having the answers as about grappling with what we believe to be the truth while living with doubt. In a society where we expect everything to work effectively and efficiently to produce heat, light, food, transport and so on, we can quickly find God at first tiresome and then irrelevant. We wrongly assume the only reason to believe in God is that he works effectively and efficiently to produce all the things that money cannot buy. His job is to provide love, peace, healing and reconciliation, a solution to global warming and an immediate communion with those we love but see no longer. Sadly for us, on these issues, he doesn't deliver; at least not in any way that we can readily understand.

At this point, we might decide to give up any idea of following Christ, in which case the riches of his great love will never challenge the shallowness of our love affair with materialism. Or we can accept the challenge to let go of a consumerist approach to faith and think more deeply about the nature of God and what his divinity asks of our humanity. For to believe in God, one has to believe in oneself. To be filled by the love of God, one has to be committed to loving oneself. To be caught up in the life of the Spirit of the universe, one has to be able to nourish the life of one's own spirit. To be in touch with God, one has to be in touch with one's own divinity. Then we can share the love of God with others and celebrate his love in creation.

Yet our desire to fall in love with Christ seems to conflict especially with our human or natural desires, which we inherit largely through our genes. In the past these desires have had the function of preserving the species. Today, left unchecked, they can cause havoc. That is not to say that all human desires, instincts and passions are deadly. We need the instinct to secure food to eat but we now realize that to do this while leaving others to die robs both them and us of life. While arguably the strongest influences on our behaviour come from our genes and other influences such as the chemical balances and imbalances of our brains, our upbringing and culture, love's fullest expression in humanity (Christ) confronts the unjust suffering of evolutionary self-preservation with self-offering love. And the greater the love we find and share, the closer we become to God who is the source of all authentic love. To be born again in this instance, therefore, is to decide to live by love rather than by our instincts.

We cannot expect our pursuit of radical love to make any significant difference to our lives when we understand it in terms of good manners or being personable with others. For divine love works at the heart of life and in human beings it challenges us to recognize and come to terms with the ways in which our natural desires either conflict or co-operate with the love of God. The word 'desire' has its roots in the Latin *de sidere* meaning 'from the stars'. So here we will take it to mean that our human desires are the stuff of creation. They are an essential part of humanity's fallen (that is, fallen from the heavens) nature. They are the driving force behind our behaviour and are part of the evolutionary inheritance of human beings from the beginning. So the love of Christ is supposed to set us free to have a greater understanding of God and a deeper sense of communion with him. Yet often we are content only to superimpose it upon our fallen human nature in such a way that it makes little difference to how we live while putting our redemption out of reach.

Whereas dark desires are the inheritance of us all, a Christian life is one in which we own these passions for ourselves and bring the love of God to bear on them in order to transform them. Sometimes we struggle with feelings of failure because we are led to believe that, being Christian, we should be able to eradicate these instincts once and for all. Most of us, however, find that the dark desires of self-preservation do not depart in peace that easily. In fact the transformation we seek usually takes time; maybe even a lifetime. It involves prayer, self-offering and service and often needs the ministry of others such as spouses, siblings, close friends, soul mates, clergy, doctors, counsellors, therapists and so on so that we can come to terms with who we are and who God calls us to be. As Eva Heymann writes, 'I can now echo words attributed to C. G. Jung: "I am not what happened to me. I am what I chose to become."'[1] So God is found at the centre of our lives where divine love and human desires compete for our interest. He is experienced at the centre of our hearts when we engage his love in a process of inner transformation that leads us to come face to face with the Christ of the world.

To highlight the way in which the Spirit confronts evolutionary driven behaviour, the chapters that follow are written in pairs where the first investigates the nature of the desire in question and the second looks at how the love of Christ challenges, re-shapes and redeems that desire. So, for example, Chapter 7 is about the desire for hatred and Chapter 8 is about the love of forgiveness.

At the end of each chapter, suggestions are made for further thought and discussion under the headings: For reflection, Something to do, A Bible passage to consider, and Prayer. This means that the book can be read by individuals or used for group work.

## Benedict and his Rule

For some years now there has been renewed interest in this Rule – written for Benedictine monks in the first half of the sixth century – as a guide for those who live outside monasteries and seek guidance on how to put their faith into practice. It is short, simple and straightforward. It is also a product of its time and we must not, therefore, take every word literally; otherwise we would, for example, consider it our duty to whip children who have made a mistake while reading a psalm and refused to show a proper degree of contrition (RB 45.1–3). Benedict drew on ideas from other Rules and is thought to have relied heavily on the 'Rule of the *Magister*', another much longer Rule in existence at the time. As a distillation of prayerful and practical guidance, Benedict's Rule contains a wealth of good advice on how we might live the Christian life and this is why it has become a source of spiritual comfort and strength for many around the world today. A Rule of Life usually regulates the life of an individual in a community and it may well be that while study of a Rule is helpful for private use, it is likely to bear further fruit when shared with others maybe in sympathy, or in company with one of the current Benedictine communities. There are references to the Rule in each chapter and suggestions for further reflection and reading are included. This, therefore, represents a brief introduction to the Rule and some of the main characteristics of Benedictine spirituality for those who would find this helpful as they grapple with their faith and lifestyle today.

I have read the Rule in a number of different English translations, all of which seem to have their own merits. For the sake of consistency, I have decided to use the one which is edited by Timothy Fry OSB from the Liturgical Press of Collegeville, Minnesota. This was first published in 1981 and is quite traditional in its style so, for example, there is no use of inclusive language. While I claim no expertise in this field, I have found that some modern translations that make the Rule more accessible, sometimes appear to miss some of the deeper nuances of the original text. I hope my use of the text offers something of interest for those who are looking for structured guidance for prayer and life or for those who are feeling a little jaded in their faith and are seeking refreshment for the soul. I have tried to put Benedict's advice in the context of a very modern struggle between humanity and divinity. I have little doubt that some of the theological reflections in this book would not have been acceptable in his time.

## *The Sayings of the Desert Fathers*

The other source of spiritual wealth and a strand that runs through much of what follows comes from a translation by Benedicta Ward of the Desert Fathers' Sayings. These, together with the writings of the other Fathers of the early Church, were a major influence on Benedict as they have been on many ever since. Again, they need to be understood in their context and some of the Sayings may at first appear rather difficult. But careful reading and study reveals a world of the early Church where the faith and practice of some of its members presents a serious challenge to our rather comfortable take on the gospel today. Probably the best known of the Desert Fathers, St Antony, is regarded by many as the founder of Western monasticism. He and many others – both men and women – in the third, fourth and fifth centuries went to live in the Egyptian – and other – deserts for a number of different reasons. Among these were the need to lead a devout, prayer-centred life without distractions, the need to escape a materialism that threatened the purity of their faith, the need to understand themselves in relation to Christ and the need to do battle with the demons that threatened to destroy them and the wider Church. They have much to teach us today and I have taken their Sayings from this one collection not least because the reader may find it helpful to read a copy of the Rule and the Sayings of the Desert Fathers alongside this book.

## *Bible reflection*

At the end of each chapter, there is a Bible passage offered for reflection which is linked to the theme of the chapter itself. The Benedictines place special importance on prayerful reflection over the Scriptures described as *lectio divina*, which we look at in the final chapter. This is one of many different ways in which to read the Bible. Whichever method we use in this context, our reading is likely to be most fruitful if we not only read the passage more than once but also:

- *stay with it* in the sense of letting it speak to us,
- *pray with it* in the sense that we enter into a dialogue with God,
- *rest in it* in the sense that we sit silently with it, taking it deep within ourselves and into our hearts, and
- *live with it* in the sense that we try and take something that we have learned from it into our daily lives.

## *Prayer*

Each chapter concludes with a prayer which can be used in a number of different ways. We can say it once, or repeat it at certain times throughout the day. We can reflect on its meaning with others before saying it together or moving on to a time of open prayer, or we can meditate on its wider meaning. However we choose to use it, to pray both at the beginning of each chapter (maybe using the prayer of the previous chapter with the Lord's Prayer) and at the end, is to offer our desires and love to God that we might be blessed in our devotion to him.

Andrew Clitherow
Lytham

# 1

## *The desire to hide*

---

There are times when the perceived lifestyle of a tortoise is extremely appealing. The tortoise is a species that has evolved in a very particular way to survive in its environment. But by projecting human qualities onto it we can invent a picture of life that can be very attractive. Such a life appeals especially to those who feel burnt out by living or working at too fast a pace or to those who have been deeply hurt in some way or another.

Watching a tortoise moving ponderously forward can make a slow pace of life seem highly desirable. This is particularly true when we are expending vast amounts of time and energy simply trying to get through each day or week. We can find ourselves in perpetual motion, looking after the children, holding down a job, doing the shopping, visiting family members, paying the mortgage, planning the holiday, arranging for a builder to fix a leaking roof, not to mention investing in our own relationships. A hard shell can also be a handy tool for those of a sensitive and caring nature who have been hurt by unkind remarks or thoughtless actions or by the suffering they see around them and on their television screens. Sensitive people sometimes find that they cope better with stress by cultivating a remote, unmoved and even uninterested air. But the most attractive feature of the lifestyle of the tortoise is the ability to retreat into a safe space at any moment, where the only person you have to worry about is yourself. The darkness here is not threatening but welcome. It restricts the sight so you don't have to worry about what you cannot see. Inside the shell it is quiet, too, so you can be at home with your own thoughts and not be disturbed by the overlapping noises and demands of other people's lives. Here in the dim light of your own presence and in the peace and quiet of your own thoughts you can rest, retreat and even sleep for ages.

To get away from the demands of life from time to time is an essential part of the lifestyle of most people. When you have a hectic lifestyle, it is often good or even essential to have a break and go on holiday. For some this may mean taking a tent to the seaside for a week while others may book themselves on a cruise or lie in the sun on a beach somewhere far away. We also provide for recreation in our weekly or monthly routines. Sporting and leisure activities can meet the need to switch off or dissipate our frustrations. Alternatively, for those of us who prefer to relax without having to engage in too much physical exercise, we may book ourselves into a therapy clinic for an Indian head massage or sauna.

But there is an enormous difference between having times when we can relax and recover a little from whatever the stresses of daily life might be and adopting a tortoise-like position because the stresses have become so great that we cannot cope any longer and the desire to run away and hide has become overwhelming. The former is part of a healthy lifestyle while the latter can be the result of too much pressure. A desire to run away can arise as a natural reaction to pain or emotional breakdown when life has gone wrong and we are no longer robust enough to take our full part in daily life. Living as if we were inside the shell of a tortoise can also be an escape that we choose because we have come to the conclusion that life outside in the world of Western material-ism is not for us. Here the shell may take the form of a small dwelling in some far flung place where we can be pretty much left alone to live as we want to. But going away does not necessarily result in a more balanced lifestyle. For when we retreat like this we can end up living only for ourselves, becoming so self-absorbed as to appear almost recklessly unconcerned about any-one else so long as we have what we want. However, it is possible to use this isolation for the good of ourselves and also for those who have not had either the calling or the opportunity to get away from it all.

Towards the end of the third century, men and women who found it impossible to be true to their Christian beliefs in what they felt was a highly secularized and materialistic society, withdrew and lived as hermits principally, though not exclusively, in the Egyptian deserts. They lived austere lives, spending their time in prayer and study of the Scriptures. Many came to them for advice and these holy men and women had an immense effect on the development of Christianity and monasticism in particular.[1] Their insights and prayers still breathe the life of the Spirit of Christ into the lungs of individual Christians today who struggle to breathe the fresh air of the gospel of Christ amid the secularized and materialistic institutional Church.

A man called Arsenius is one of the better known of these early hermits. He was an educated Roman nobleman who had spent some time in the Emperor's court in Rome. Once when a fellow monk asked him for advice he replied, 'As far as possible, try hard to make your inner progress as God would have it, and by this overcome the passions of the body.' He also said, 'If we seek God, he will appear to us; if we grasp Him, He will stay with us.'[2]

Here we can see that Arsenius' desire to hide came from his longing to develop his inner spiritual life according to the will of God. In so doing he aimed to master the inner desires – common to most human beings – that impede the development of the love of God in us. And we can understand this to be the principal aim of all those who withdrew to the desert at this time. The 'passions' or desires he refers to are such things as a lack of self-control, anger, the desire to judge others, to give in to harmful sexual desire and practice, to over-indulge in what we eat and drink and to live for ourselves, forgetting about God and everyone else.

The desire to hide, therefore, can lead to a withdrawal from society that draws us into a deeper engagement with ourselves and the world, which leads us ultimately into a deeper communion with God. This is the background and basis of Benedictine spirituality. In fact, society is constantly enriched whenever it accepts the wisdom of those who reflect on life from this perspective, whether their thoughts come from a desert place or from a hermitage in the backyard of a house near a city centre. Such wisdom inevitably leads to a deeper appreciation and experience of love, the basis of all appreciation of the God of creative love from whom the universe has its origins.

But when we cave in as a result of too much pressure or pain, or when we have suffered a breakdown or our lives have fallen apart for some unexpected reason, the inside of a shell can become an attractive place to hide. Here we can pretend that we no longer need to engage with mainstream life in any way. This is also a place where those who have been made to feel unloved and unlovable can hide in the undemanding environs of the anonymity to which they have been reduced. Unfortunately, such isolation in itself seldom helps us rediscover our self-confidence. And it is unlikely to promote the inner progress that releases the love of God that alone can draw us to a deeper appreciation of the significance of our lives both in the here and now and in the greater scheme of things.

When the desire to run away and hide, either a part or the whole of ourselves, becomes overwhelming, we need to reassure ourselves – or others we know who have hidden themselves away – that this is likely to be a very natural reaction to what we are experiencing. Hiding has always been a device used by human beings to protect and preserve themselves and those to whom they are related or depend upon. It is an instinct we share with animals. When we are attacked we can choose to fight or run away or if that is not an option, we can hide. Children at play often learn skills that they will need for real in later life. They can play a game in which they all run away from one of their number designated as the 'catcher' who then chases them. The game of hide-and-seek, where one or more run away and hide while the 'catcher' waits with eyes closed before going to try and find the others, is still popular today. As youngsters, therefore, we can learn how to manage the 'fight or flight' instinct which can preserve us from harm later on in life.

However, the desire to shut down the mind or the emotions when hurt or under pressure can take place both as the result of a conscious decision on our part because of a perceived threat and as an automatic response at an instinctive and unconscious level in the mind. Sometimes when the mind is in overload we suddenly become aware – often through something that someone else has said to us – that it seems to have shut out anything it cannot cope with so that we can deal with demands one at a time. Again, these are natural responses that are part of our inherited human nature. But while natural desires can lead to our adopting survival patterns of behaviour whereby we engage less than fully in daily life, they do not always provide ways to help us re-engage in a balanced and fulfilling way once the threat to ourselves has disappeared. So, while our minds may shut down to some degree when under pressure, it may take more than the later recovery of mental equilibrium to help us restore faith in ourselves and in others.

This is one of those instances where our human desires, our natural love and the love of God need to work together. While ultimately all come from God in creation, our instinctive desires and human love – love that consciously or unconsciously expects some kind of return at little cost to ourselves – are both a natural part of our human nature. The love of God, on the other hand, while inherent in creation and in human beings, comes as a gift of grace to those who are prepared to embark on the way of divine love. This involves a commitment to love as God loves, sacrificially if need be for the sake of the other, and without conditions. Our human love and our desires work sympathetically together to produce goodness. But when they co-operate with divine love they lead to godliness, thereby advancing our inner progress towards God. To seek or hold on to God in this way is to discover him staying with us. In this context Benedictine spirituality can be described as 'bringing the uniqueness in us and around us to holiness'.[3]

So as we accept that our natural desire for self-preservation leads us to hide from time to time, we can also understand that in order to emerge from the darkness we need to allow the love of God to work on us. As we saw in the Introduction, it is a mistake to think that the love of God, and in particular the divine love that we see in Jesus Christ, is at all times diametrically opposed to our human desires. Many desires are dangerous for our long-term health and well-being. They originate from inherited patterns of behaviour passed from generation to generation through our genes or cultural traditions for our short-term benefit. So in order to take responsibility for our lives, we have to understand that to live purely by such desires is to put ourselves, and those closest to us, first at all times while ignoring the welfare of others. And as our desires prompt us to put our own interests first, we forget how far away we are from any kinds of relationship whereby we could honestly say that we love others – our neighbours – as we love ourselves. In fact, this is how most of us experience life and love, that is, in the contaminated environment of worldly existence where good and evil seem to be inextricably bound together most of the time. Left to ourselves, we tend to live much more according to our human nature rather than by sacrificial love.

By contrast, God's developing plan for creation is for Divine love to work increasingly on our fallen desires – not to eliminate them in all circumstances but to increase the purposes of Divine love, to transform them to produce godly people and through them a healed and healing society. And the Church at its best is supposed to offer an environment where we can learn what this means and how best we might go about it. As Timothy Radcliffe observes,

> Most people think of religion as about the control of desire. Desire is dangerous and disturbing and so religion helps us tame it. But traditionally this has not been the teaching of the Church. We are invited to deepen our desires, to touch their hidden hunger, to liberate desire in recognition of its ultimate gaol.[4]

The ultimate goal here is the healing of those whose natural desire has been to hide so that they can come out of the protective environment they have created for themselves – or that others have forced them into – to have the faith to be themselves.

So if we have hidden ourselves away from others, or if we have shut up parts of ourselves because we dare not be hurt again, what can we do to emerge from the restrictions of our protective shell? Arsenius' advice seems to be that if we are to make the inner progress that both we and God want for ourselves, we have first of all to dedicate ourselves to learn how transforming love can lead us to God.

For the Christian this takes place primarily through our relationship with Jesus Christ. To come out of our shell, therefore, is to be prepared to find where Christ can live within us. For the desire to be with others is none other than the desire to be with Christ.

Someone once told Jesus that they would follow him wherever he went. He replied, 'Foxes have holes, and birds of the air have nests; but the Son of Man has nowhere to lay his head.'[5] From this response we might surmise that the person who asked the question was someone who was very settled in his life and had no intention of changing his lifestyle or moving his life around in order to make the kind of inner progress that Jesus calls for. He was stuck where he was. He may even have been someone whose desire had been to hide a part or all of himself away. Here the challenge is clear. If you want to move out of the darkness into the light, you have to actively opt into the love of Christ. Having done so, there will be many things that can assist in the healing process, such as developing one's prayer life and rediscovering one's identity as a child of God.

When we have become unhappy with the way in which we have adopted our own hiding places, it is not sufficient to say we want to change and to learn about love again. We have to search for divine love or, as Arsenius says, 'we have to seek and take hold of God'. Only then we can move forward, although it is likely that in the initial stages, our gait may still be slow and ponderous like that of a tortoise. It will also take time for our eyes to adjust when we move from a place that is dark to a place bathed in light, and it takes time for us to build up our confidence when we learn to re-engage with life. But progress can be made if behind each step there is the commitment to move on in life and in our relationships.

\* \* \*

## *From the Rule of St Benedict*

In his prologue to the Rule, Benedict offers the following advice to those who are considering following Christ through being a member of a Benedictine community:

> Let us get up then, at long last, for the Scriptures rouse us when they say: 'It is high time for us to arouse from sleep.'[6] Let us open our eyes to the light that comes from God, and our ears to the voice from heaven that every day calls out this charge: 'If you hear his voice today, do not harden your hearts.'[7] (RB Prologue 8–10)

This reminds us that it is never too late to deal with the things that restrict our self-expression and development. We are given times in our lives to deal with issues that keep us in the dark but we have to be sufficiently awake and open to recognize them for what they are, namely opportunities to grow not just in goodness but in godliness, too.

## *For reflection*

Take time to consider whether there are parts of your life in which you have decided to hide yourself from others to the detriment of yourself. What is it exactly that you are hiding? Can you work out what caused you to hide like this? Do you think it is time to do something about it? Are you going to harden your heart and stay stubbornly where you are or are you prepared to commit yourself to moving on? Do you need a break? Is it time to book a holiday or retreat?

## Something to do

If you want to stop hiding all or part of yourself, think about who can help you move forward with this. This may be a member of your family, or a close friend. Arrange to have an initial discussion with them – in confidence if need be – and then move on to talk about how you might bring the love of God to bear on your desire to hide.

## A Bible passage to consider

> Again Jesus spoke to them, saying, 'I am the light of the world. Whoever follows me will never walk in darkness but will have the light of life.' (John 8.12)

## Prayer

> Dear God of Universal Light, if my life is meant to include a journey of inner progress according to your will, grant me the wisdom to recognize your way, the desire to move out of my shell and the love that will lead me to you.

# 2

## *The love of God*

The title of this chapter refers both to the love that God has for us and also to the love that we can have for him. Christians believe that these two loves are, in fact, one.

So what kind of love does God have for us? If we imagine that God loves in the same way as we sometimes love others, we might wonder why on earth he would love someone as unlovely or ordinary as ourselves. But then our love is not always sacrificial or limitless in its nature. In addition to our understanding of the love that God has for us and the authentic love that we might develop through faith in God, our first experience of love is usually the power to love that we inherit as part of our human nature. It is centred on the care of those closest to us so as to ensure our survival and theirs. Natural love, therefore, usually comes with conditions. But the love of which human nature is capable can lead through faith and sacrifice to the love of God involving us in the Divine life of creation.

In natural love great importance is placed on the desire for self-preservation where there are limits to what we are prepared to put up with. This is the seedbed for Divine love, but the full flower of self-offering and unconditional love – planted in the heart by God – does not always flourish here. The two loves can feel very similar, but natural love is powered mostly by the emotions and human interest whereas Divine love energized by the Spirit of God – seen most vividly in the Spirit of Christ – touches the emotions but is grounded in God. Human love is susceptible to the effect of our natural reaction to pain whereas Divine love is more likely to absorb pain – even seeking it out at times – in order to redeem it. In between the love of human nature and the love of God stands the cross, beckoning us to go beyond ourselves and our self-interest into self-giving love. In marked contrast to our withdrawal into the safety of ourselves when we are hurt by love, the cross beckons us to meet pain and confusion with self-offering even, or especially, when our survival and perhaps the survival of others are at risk.

According to natural love, sometimes what we had considered to be strong and mature relationships can suffer irreparable damage when one partner does or says something that causes deep pain in the other. An ultimatum is given and when that mistake is repeated, the relationship suffers. Either it is terminated by the one who feels he or she has been offended against, or both parties decide – usually without too much discussion – to stay together but to hide a part or parts of themselves from the other. If, for example, someone says that you are lousy in bed, your hurt can make you decide to keep to yourself in future or seek solace in someone else. In a heavily consumer-orientated society, the need of someone who bought into a relationship to then get out of it – or to opt out of parts of it – only because it is not paying expected dividends in terms of happiness and security, can result in unnecessarily fractured lives and broken love. In among the broken bits and pieces of such relationships, sacrificial love beckons us to go beyond the limitations of human love and patience, to a deeper understanding of love that leads to the healing of the human spirit.

When our natural human love does not lead us to the love of God, we are diminished and society is characterized by its selfishness. As a consequence, we can end up losing faith not only in ourselves but also in God. For if we are more casual and less committed to our love for others, we don't feel we need to bother to accept or begin to appreciate the love of God. When we are content to love only as far as our human nature will take us, we find the concept of a God of love unworkable and unfeasible. But when we commit – at no little cost to ourselves – to the way of sacrificial love, we can begin to see the traces of divine love among the broken bits and pieces of our relationships and in creation.

Through the life and teaching of Jesus Christ, we can see that the nature of God is not primarily judgemental but loving and forgiving. St John puts it like this:

> For God so loved the world that he gave his only Son, so that everyone who believes in him may not perish but may have eternal life. Indeed, God did not send the Son into the world to condemn the world, but in order that the world might be saved through him.[1]

In other words, the love of God is unconditional and assured. He does not want to judge and condemn us. On the contrary, he wants us to live as full a life as possible by being close to him. And this love of God not only brings new meaning to our lives and helps us understand where our real identity lies – why we are here and what we are meant to do – it also has a healing effect sometimes on our bodies, usually on our minds and invariably on our spirits.

We have seen that desire (*de-sire*, literally 'of the stars') is both dangerous and exciting stuff, for it contains our fallen desires and ambitions while also holding within it the divine power of creation. While a human being left to his or her own devices will always revert to the laws of human nature as it has emerged through the evolutionary process, human becoming happens when that instinctual behaviour is redeemed by Divine love. It is the will of God that we take responsibility for our lives and in particular for the way we love, so that through the redemption of our fallen desires the world might fall back in love with him.

We invest heavily in the proclamation of Jesus as the Son of God because by doing so we have a way to understand how much God loves us. He loves us so much, he did not spare his own Son. Get it? God offers himself in his love for us to the extent that he will take on the greatest suffering of the world in order to lead it back to himself. But when we ask ourselves why God should love us so much, we tend to measure the love of God only by the parameters of our natural love. As a result, our understanding of his love is going to fall a long way short of what it is meant to be.

When we fall in love with another human being and allow our life to be shaped by theirs – just as their life is shaped by ours – we can be left initially in a state of disbelief that someone could love us so much. And this doesn't necessarily change when you've been with someone for many years, experienced many things, struggled through difficult times and celebrated many happy occasions. Still at the end of the day when you lay your head on the pillow, you sense that you are the luckiest person in the world because of the continuing and constant love and commitment of your partner lying contentedly next to you. Sometimes on a birthday or wedding anniversary, or writing a Christmas card, our loved ones may feel moved to try and put into words why it is they love us so much. But if ever we ask them why they love us, the question can be followed by a long silence. This is not necessarily because they do not love us or cannot think of anything to say (at least we hope not) but because there comes a point when words won't suffice. We just end up saying, 'I love you because I do and that's it.' This is because, in addition to those things we might want to write on cards, there is something indefinable that is just 'there'. But it is here that we can discover our destiny. As John O'Donohue writes, 'There is an awakening between you, a sense of ancient knowing. Love opens the door of ancient recognition. You enter. You come home to each other at last. As Euripides says, "Two friends, one soul".'2 For this degree of loving commitment defies description. What is more, such love has a healing effect on us by helping us to believe in ourselves in all circumstances and by its constant encouragement of us to fulfil our potential. This is a process that lasts as long as we are together, it does not happen usually as a quick fix. We are not healed of all our fears and foibles straightaway. The process usually takes time.

It is difficult, however, to know the love of God in this way if we do not at the same time know ourselves. If we have hidden ourselves behind a role that we habitually play or behind a mask we put on in the morning that disguises who we really are, this can be another reason why we can struggle to find God. St Augustine, one of the greatest writers and thinkers in the history of the Church,[3] in his need to confess to God his wayward thinking and lifestyle before he became a Christian says, 'But where was I when I looked for you? You were there before my eyes, but I had deserted even my own self. I could not find myself, much less find you.'[4] But there is more to the development of a dawning realization of the love of God than even this degree of self-acceptance.

The early Christians sometimes referred to 'seeing with the eyes of the heart'. I take it that they meant that while we can see the world around us through our eyes and reflect on what we can see, when we communicate with God through our spirits, we do this from the seat of love and eternity within ourselves that can be described as the heart of ourselves. 'Blessed are the pure in heart for they will see God,'[5] Jesus says and he also encourages his disciples to love God with all their heart, mind and spirit and to love their neighbours as they love themselves.[6] It is as if he is saying that in order to love others we need to know how to love – or unconditionally accept – ourselves. So our ability to see God is in proportion to our willingness to focus our hearts on him together with our commitment to love others. For it makes no sense if we say that we love God who loves everyone equally and then either put conditions on our acceptance of others or even write some of them off as undesirable. While it would be much easier if we could keep it to ourselves, our acceptance of the love of God cannot be a private affair.

To apprehend the love of God in this way, is surely far too difficult in a world that has fallen so deeply in love with itself. If my ability to ascertain and appreciate the love of God depends upon a deep love of myself and others, it is unlikely that I shall be able to apprehend the love of God to any great degree. For it is more than likely that at any one time I shall not be as self-aware as I should be, or that I have fallen out with my neighbours or colleagues at work, or that I have forgotten about God for a while. The result of this will be that my appreciation of Divine love is likely to be partial or non-existent for most of the time.

Given our knowledge of human nature, this is both a logical and natural conclusion. But for most people – and sometimes for the greatest of saints – seeing God through a glass darkly is about as much as we shall see in this life. It may not sound much, but it is enough to get us through. For often it is when our lives are in a mess or when we have been hurt and part of us is in hiding or kept in the dark, that we discover we are closer to God than ever. For while we might withdraw from seemingly pointless relationships or painful situations, a faithful God cannot walk away from his creation when it wanders away from him. God is far more faithful to us than we are to him. St Augustine remarks, 'I call upon you, O God, my Mercy, who made me and did not forget me when I forgot you.'[7] So sometimes when we call out to God from the shadows of our confusion, or hear his voice calling us out of our self-imposed darkness, we are closer to him than ever.

We might wonder from time to time whether it's worth bothering with all of this. We tend to live increasingly busy and demanding lives. We have weighty responsibilities both at work and at home. Muddling through is what we do best. Most of the time, it is all we can do. How do we hold all these competing demands together? We might feel that we do not have time to work on our desires, natural love and divine love and so on. In times past, there was a day of the week when most things stopped and most people had time to reflect on such things if they wanted to, but that luxury seems to have largely disappeared.

All, however, is not lost. In the Prologue to his Rule, St Benedict reminds his followers 'to regulate their lives' – this includes both those who live in religious communities and those who do not – that when the demands of the Christian life seem too much, we should ask for help, 'What is not possible to us by nature, let us ask the Lord to supply by the help of his grace' (RB Prologue 41). And in this instance, the grace we need to ask for is the prayer of attentiveness that we may begin to apprehend the love of God and the glory of his presence in our daily lives.

We may think that prayer is for some but not for others and usually not for ourselves. But we can learn how to pray in many different ways and it is important to find the way of personal prayer that is right for us in the present. (This may be a different form of prayer than the one we learned as children.) The prayer of attentiveness is one of the easier forms of prayer. For it is not something we do but rather a state of being spiritually aware of the presence of the Spirit of the creator God in the universe and in Jesus Christ. It comes to us not as a result of our own efforts but as a gift to those who ask, and it consists most of all in a desire to be obedient to God.

Towards the end of the Prologue, St Benedict says that in order to live in God's presence, we must 'prepare our hearts and bodies for the battle of holy obedience to his instructions' (RB Prologue 40). And Syncletica, the abbess of one of the first Christian monasteries once said, 'It seems to me that for those who live in monasteries obedience is a higher virtue than chastity, however perfect. Chastity is in danger of pride, obedience has the promise of humility.'[8]

At a time when self-expression and the freedom of the individual are highly cherished, obedience sounds old fashioned and something that is likely to crush individuality, but here it really means attentive listening. The word for obedience which is widely used throughout the New Testament implies primarily the importance of listening and responding to what one hears. St Benedict clearly thinks it lies at the heart of the spiritual life. He begins the Prologue with the words, 'Listen carefully, my son, to the master's instructions, and attend to them with the ear of your heart' (RB Prologue 1). Thereafter, in the next 50 verses that precede the Rule itself, he refers 4 times to the need to obey and no less than 11 times to the need to listen.

So the prayer of obedience, or we might refer to it as the prayer of attentiveness, is of vital importance for our spiritual progress.

But what are we meant to be attentive to? The most straight-forward answer to this would be to say that we need to listen to the word of God in our reading of the Bible, in the Rule of St Benedict, in the mouths of those whom we meet and in creation. It may not be possible to listen to so much all at once but it is important to begin to listen or to rediscover the art of listening to God for he 'speaks' to us in many different ways. For the most part, this form of listening is a prayer of unspoken dialogue between divine and human spirit. In the Bible, there are a number of verses where our ability to listen to the voice of God is determined by the condition of our hearts as the seat of our emotions, understanding and spirit. And the heart of our being, at our centre or in our inner being, is where the Divine promise for our life is changed into the transforming presence of God deep within us. So when Benedict asks us to listen with the 'ear of our heart' he is asking us to be attentive to God in a way that will have a deep effect on who we are and what we do. For Christian vocation is first of all to do with who we have been called to be and then with what we have been called to do. We often make the mistake of starting with the second because we think it is going to be easier when in fact living the Christian life can only be achieved as the result of a transfiguring process in the heart of ourselves.

In the prayer of attentiveness, we don't need to say anything out loud nor are we likely to hear anything out loud. But by attentive listening, we look for the word of love in creation – where natural love gives way to Divine love – which we may come across through our appreciation of the natural world or through words of love spoken to us or to someone we know. By raising our spiritual awareness in this way, either in times when we are still or as we go about our daily lives, we can begin to become more aware of God and what he is 'saying' to us and of a connectedness between our spirit and the Spirit of God.

We may not find this easy to begin with and it may take a while to move into this prayer of attentiveness, but if we can manage to do this to some degree, it is likely that we will begin to find the love of God drawing us closer to him. And in a way, the rest of this book is about different ways in which we can respond to that love.

\* \* \*

## From the Rule of St Benedict

St Benedict is both firm and gentle with those who want to follow his Rule. He understands that it is not easy to develop a Christian way of life to begin with and encourages us to persevere through the tough times.

> The good of all concerned, however, may prompt us to a little strictness in order to amend faults and to safeguard love. Do not be daunted immediately by fear and run away from the road that leads to salvation. It is bound to be narrow at the outset. (RB Prologue 47–48)

## For reflection

Set some time aside to think about those areas of your life where your love for others is important. Think about those closest to you to whom you have made a deep commitment. Then think about others whom you love (that is, those you want nothing but the best for in all circumstances because of your personal relationship with them) who may be your more distant relatives, workmates or friends. Give yourself plenty of time to do this and as you do, try and work out where in your relationships your love is conditional on what you need to receive yourself and where it is unconditional and sacrificial. Be as honest with yourself as you can. Having done this, take time to give thanks for the love of which you are aware and where you are blessed in giving or receiving unconditional, sacrificial love. Give thanks for this presence of God in your life and in the life of others. Finally, look at those areas where your needs are getting in the way of your ability to give or receive authentic love. See if there are any ways in which Divine love can further transform the love of your selfish needs.

## Something to do

Try and develop your daily awareness of the presence of God. Try not to do this by suddenly deciding to make assumptions about where you 'see' God when in fact you do not. The idea behind listening with the ear of your heart is to engage your spirit more than your intellect with creation.

One way we can do this is to choose a time of day, maybe going to work or in our lunch hour, to pause and look at the way we are looking at the world. Most of the time, we look with a view to seeing where we are going or what we are doing. But try instead to look at less for a while but look at it differently in the sense that you are looking at it not for what you need from it but for what it is in its own right, what it would be if you were not there. Having done this, think about how God might regard what you are looking at.

Another way is to spend time sitting still, closing our eyes, breathing deeply, allowing our breath to descend into our hearts and developing an awareness in the heart of our selves. This takes time and practice, but after a while it is possible to look at the world through the 'heart of our selves'. This technique is likely (though not exclusively) to work better for introverts than for extroverts.

Or you might like to take a Bible passage, like the one below or some other, or a verse from the Rule of St Benedict, and spend time thinking about what you think you can 'hear' God saying to you through it. Or you might like to remember something that someone has said to you recently that you feel is of particular significance for your spiritual development and see what God is saying to you through their words. Remember that the prayer of attentiveness – when our heart is closer than usual to the heart of God – also involves being attentive to the voice of God in our daily life. This is where the 'change in our behaviour' part of obedience comes into play.

## A Bible passage to consider

God is love, and those who abide in love abide in God, and God abides in them. (1 John 4.16)

## Prayer

Loving God,
may I have the grace
to be attentive to your word,
to have a heart full of your love
and the courage to follow in your way.
Amen.

# 3

## *The desire to fulfil the dreams of others*

———◆◆◆———

Towards the end of my time at school, when I was preparing to take my A Level examinations, I can remember being envious of one of my school friends with whom I had spent a lot of time over the previous five years. He lived by the sea and during his holidays enjoyed studying the shipping, which he could see from his bedroom window. As a result, he had developed a very keen interest in the Royal Navy. In fact, he had an encyclopaedic knowledge of its ships, even remembering the length and tonnage of each vessel. His one desire in life was to join the Royal Navy. Everyone knew of his great obsession so, unsurprisingly, his nickname was 'Admiral' and though unoriginal, it suited him well.

I envied him because as we were preparing for our final public exams and looking to a future beyond school, I didn't have much of a clue about what might lie ahead whereas 'Admiral' knew exactly what he wanted to do. It was likely that I would apply to join the Army but I didn't really know what I wanted to do with my life. While I have encouraged my own children not to worry if at the end of full-time education they are not sure what it is they want to do, at their age I was impatient. I wanted the security of knowing what lay ahead. I wanted to survive. Self-preservation demanded I find a role so that I might compete with others who fitted more easily into the system. While I was content to sit light to it for a while, I knew I would have to opt in to the system sometime.

Having been told early on that I was not intelligent enough to pass any examination of significance, I was surprised when I discovered I had gained good enough grades at A Level to go to university. So at the last minute, while I knew nothing about it, I decided to study Theology because at the time I was interested in Jesus Christ. It was only when I began to study for my degree that I realized there was a great deal more to the course than studying the life and teaching of Jesus Christ. It was quite a shock. While this was going on, 'Admiral' was accepted for officer training in the Royal Navy where he has remained all his working life. I don't think he has achieved the rank which we conferred on him in the Sixties but by all accounts he has had a good time. I went off to university and through an indirect route and much to my astonishment, ended up being ordained.

From a superficial point of view, the 'Admiral's' life might appear pretty predictable, whereas mine was not. He works in the Ministry of Defence while I am a parish priest living on the Fylde Coast. I would guess, however, that while his desire was clear and mine was not, neither of us really had any idea of how things might turn out. Looking back I can see that it was right for him to pursue his dream from a very early age and it was also right for me to take a more circuitous route to discover my way ahead but either way, on both our journeys, consciously or unconsciously, we will have had to answer the question, 'Who do you desire to be?' We tend to ask young people 'what' rather than 'who' they are going to be because often the role we have dictates – at least in the minds of others – a raft of assumptions and expectations about us based on their understanding of what we do. We might desire to become a nurse or a builder, a soldier or a surveyor and while we can find these roles suit our personalities they can also have a strong influence on how we regard ourselves as we go about our daily living.

So another reason why I envied 'Admiral' at school was that his clear idea concerning what he was going to do gave him, in my eyes, not only a destiny that had to be fulfilled but also an identity. But I made the mistake of confusing what he was going to do with who he was going to be. Since then I have come to realize that while we have to decide what we are going to do with our lives in terms of employment, marriage, lifestyle, family and so on (this may change at any number of points when we might seek or have forced upon us a career change or an alternative way of life), we have also to decide who we are going to be in order to find peace within ourselves. And it doesn't take long to find out that usually it is far more demanding to embark on the personal development trail than it is to secure a good job and career.

The other day someone who has struggled all her life with the demands of overbearing parents – whose desire was to keep her permanently on a tight lead – said to me that following the death of her father, she had come to realize that she felt she had lost at least 30 years of her life, trying to live up to the false expectations of her parents. Now married and with grown-up children, she desires nothing other than to be herself and to have the freedom to do what she wants for the rest of her life. I wonder sometimes how she copes with knowing that the abusive relationship she suffered at the hands of her parent cheated her (her words) of some of the best years of her life. It would be understandable if she became angry and resentful although I have been surprised by the number of people who 'lose' years of their lives in this or some other similar way but are able to forget and forgive, and move on. But sadly, this is not always the case. Recently I received a phone call late at night from someone who was clearly tormented by the abuse he had experienced as a child and was struggling to come to terms with it. For now, above all, he is driven by a desire for justice so that he can achieve some degree of closure over the whole sad episode.

So sometimes when we ask ourselves, 'Who do we think we are?' we can become aware of ways in which instead of concentrating on being ourselves, we have spent years of our lives – consciously or unconsciously – desiring to live up to the expectations, or having our behaviour dictated by the actions, of others. This may not be because of such extreme cases of abuse but simply because we chose the wrong career or partner or because we have never been aware of some of the influences on us when we were young. Or maybe early on in our lives, during a formative period, we have taken on the values and perspectives of society without working out what effect they might have on us. A government's drive for high employment figures may have conspired to our pushing ourselves – or being pushed by others – into a way of life or career almost for the sake of it without much freedom of choice. In fact, childhood or the teenage years for many are often far from perfect times of personal development when we lay the foundations for a balanced happy life in the future. Parenting seems to be such an inexact art that it can take some of us a long time to unravel the conflicting strands of parental expectations. Coming to terms with adulthood does not take place at the same stage of life for everyone. Few of us become fully aware of ourselves and our potential the day we become 18. Add to this, peer pressure and a lack of self-awareness, and for some it can take years of adult reflection to discover their true selves.

There are, of course, those who think developing this level of self-awareness is a waste of time. They end up inflicting similar wounds on others to those that they themselves received. 'It was good enough for me so it's good enough for them' is their motto. But, referring to St Luke's Gospel, Benedict also says that we should pursue humility by never thinking of ourselves as being more important than we are for 'every exaltation is a kind of pride'. Quoting the Psalmist, he says that we should not 'go after marvels beyond ourselves' (RB 7.2–3). For by having false dreams or ambitions we are not only likely to make ourselves unhappy, we are also inclined to put ourselves above our need of God.

If there is such a thing as original sin that is passed on from one generation to the next in the way that the sins of Adam become the sins of the human race, I reckon that this is best illustrated in the way most people accumulate emotional and psychological baggage in their childhood and upbringing from their parents or others. Even with the best intentions we cannot prevent imbalance or a distortion of our understanding of ourselves creeping in at some stage or other. While life can seldom be described as a state of perfect bliss, we need at some moment in our lives to come to terms with those aspects of ourselves that constrain our freedom. We do this so that we can reach a point where we can enjoy balanced relationships and a sense of fulfilment about who we are. Often this task of befriending these shadows cast across our souls falls to our spouses, partners or close friends who usually know us better than we know ourselves.

I am not suggesting that we are all neurotic or psychologically damaged. Far from it. But few of us can avoid accumulating the odd chip on the shoulder or distorted view of ourselves or others from time to time. Human relationships are imperfect at best and all worthwhile relationships require both commitment and hard work, usually on an on-going basis. And while not everyone has suffered the effects of child abuse of one kind or another, we can sometimes discover that we have embarked on a way of life because of the direct or indirect influence of someone else rather than as a result of our own free choice. We might be very successful in our work or very settled at home but on occasions it is as if we wake up to realize that the usual clothes we have been wearing for years don't fit any more. In fact, we suspect they haven't been right for ages. So we begin to think about how we can move on.

If as you read this you feel you do not need to confront any of these issues in your life, you may like to consider if there are others around you who may be struggling in this kind of way, who may also be looking to you for support. It is worth remembering that the influences and experiences that distort our understanding of ourselves do not occur only in our childhood and upbringing. They can occur at any stage of life.

Of course, we can continue as we are and not bother facing up to any distorted images of who we are. In many ways it is less demanding if we simply say life is unjust and unfair and there is a sense in which we are all products of our past – or someone else's – and that's the way it is. But in doing so, we may well find that we feel less than fulfilled in our lives or in our relationships, and by not coming to terms with who we are, we may well inflict our unease on others. And if we are not very careful, our religion becomes a way in which our unbalanced understanding of who we are is falsely legitimized rather than confronted for the fake that it is. Our Christian understanding of ourselves is that we have all been made in the image of God. This means that we have also been called to rediscover this image when we realize it has been distorted by misplaced love, unresolved resentment or deliberate abuse in ourselves and others. Being made in the image of God involves learning how our desire to find our own way in life needs to be balanced by a desire to learn how to love without the distortions of other people's false expectations or our misplaced perceptions of who we should be.

Reading the Rule of St Benedict today, we might be forgiven for thinking that he seems to suggest we should be quite hard on ourselves. Some might think that these exhortations are more likely to crush individuality than help it to blossom. 'Renounce your self in order to follow Christ (Matt 16.24; Luke 9.23)', he says and 'discipline your body (1 Cor 9.27); do not pamper yourself, but love fasting' (RB 4.10–12). Unfashionable though these exhortations are, they remind us how much we have to struggle against the love of excess that is so much a part of our daily life if we are to develop any kind of love for ourselves and others in a godly way. He reminds us also that the way to self-discovery and individual freedom is not through acquisition but by self-denial. To have the freedom to love someone else, we have to be free of ambitions and roles we assume that prevent us from loving ourselves. To this we will return in the next chapter.

All authentic faith should help us discover how we can love God and also how we can love our neighbours as ourselves.[1] For some the idea that we should love ourselves smacks too much of self-indulgence. This can be the result of a poor level of self-understanding, for to love oneself is to be self-aware rather than self-centred. When we are aware of our strengths and weaknesses, we are less likely to mistreat our children in a similar way to which our parents made mistakes with us. We also become aware of the prejudices and fears that sometimes haunt our dealings with others whom we perceive to be a threat to our existence and future. Unfortunately we frequently forget that love of oneself – that is, the self-acceptance of ourselves as having been made in the image of God – precedes our love of others. So the degree to which we find love in our own hearts and adopt this as the basis of our lives usually determines the degree to which we are free to love others.

So when our *locus of evaluation* is found somewhere external to our inner self, personal identity is exchanged to a greater or lesser degree for the need to live up to the images and expectations of others.[2]

Without this desired level of self-awareness someone who, for example, has been brought up in an environment where there is much overt criticism of anyone who is perceived to deviate from what is regarded as respectable behaviour, is likely to define their faith in these terms as well. Those who have been subjected to sharp judgemental attitudes themselves at a formative time in their lives, are likely to become judgemental of others in the way they express their religious faith. Here the 'oughts', 'shalls' and 'shall nots' particularly of Old Testament legal codes are seized upon to confirm the distorted images and haunt those on whom the self-righteous inflict them. These lists of prohibitions can seriously inhibit our development. While they can serve an important function in producing a form of social cohesion and ordered society, they can also make us think 'I ought to pretend to be someone else otherwise I shall not be acceptable to my fellow believers or to God.' Human becoming cannot happen when religious leaders

burden others with guilt and self-denial for simply being themselves, with the threat of hell and damnation thrown in for good
measure. So we become afraid of the part of ourselves we hide
from others and we end up defining who we are by saying 'I ought'
rather than 'I am'. (This, of course, is not restricted to the abuse
of the Christian faith alone.)

'The kingdom of God is within you' says Jesus.[3] Because we
believe that God is to be found deep within all of us, it is at these
depths that we have been called to have a dialogue with the
Divine source of life. When we possess an unenlightened view
of ourselves, we are likely to resort to judgements and decisions
made for us by others or by our church leaders. Because we have
become so out of touch with our inner selves, we dare not make
our own decisions for fear of getting them wrong. So those who
have been brought up to believe in a traditional theistic image
of God, find the formal religious rites and rituals provide them
with all the justification they need to promote their agenda for
survival – which comes usually at the expense of someone else –
and to treat others in a way that is less compassionate than how
they would expect to be treated themselves.

When our distorted images of ourselves and others are con-
firmed either by the selection of friends or spouses or indeed our
faith community – which again we might inherit from misplaced
influences in our past – we conform to patterns of behaviour
formed by our natural instincts. We cannot cope well with the
challenge of those who are different from ourselves because they
make us aware of the fragility of our own misunderstanding of
human nature. They also threaten our survival. As a result we
often resort to the spirituality of self-justification as our inner
self or spirit struggles to have any kind of deep relationship with
God.

So when we take away these false external *loci of evaluation*, those
who define themselves by them may well be left, initially at least,
feeling very ill at ease with life, and personally threatened. As a

result they might lash out in hatred against those who challenge the prejudice that has become their companion and soul mate. On the other hand, they may accept the challenge to review their desire to be themselves and discover a new freedom and fulfilment in owning their own life.

By now, we can see how easy it is for the demons of religious prejudice to define our behaviour and also our understanding of ourselves. But when we are unaware of this, while we still believe we are representing the Christ of respectable religion in an evil world, we have ourselves become the cause of alienation and division. This chaotic – sometimes lethal – mess of inner dislocation is common to many both inside faith communities and outside who find other creeds in which to believe and sustain a suspect spirituality today.

It doesn't, then, take a great leap of imagination to see how the Christian faith, for example, can be used to perpetuate these values for the supposed glory of God, whereas Jesus – who in his time could never be described as a model of respectable behaviour – calls us not to be judgemental in our attitudes and dealings with others.[4] The fullness of Christian life is defined by our ability to have the faith to be ourselves and to allow others to be themselves, too.

\* \* \*

## *From the Rule of St Benedict*

Your way of acting should be different from the world's way; the love of Christ must come before all else. You are not to act in anger or nurse a grudge. Rid your heart of all deceit. Never give a hollow greeting of peace or turn away when someone needs your love. Bind yourself to no oath lest it prove false, but speak the truth with heart and tongue. (RB 4.20–28)

## *For reflection*

Instead of asking questions concerning who we think we are, we should ask who our lives belong to. Does my life belong to me or to my parents, educators, the political leaders of my country, to those who are my managers at work, to my wife or husband or to anyone other than myself? Is it my life or theirs? Where have I negotiated joint ownership in order to survive and contribute to society and where have others taken my liberty from me?

Do you feel powerless and need to rediscover the power to be yourself?

What is your dream of who you are? How much of that dream are you living?

## Something to do

If you are aware of areas of your life where your relationships with others are suffering because you are not being true to yourself, let alone to them, try and find a way to be more honest with yourself.

If your faith in God helps you confirm your prejudices about others, or if your church encourages you to be judgemental about others, try and work out ways in which this might be changed for good.

Give thanks to God for those who give you identity and meaning in a positive and creative way because of their love for you. Wherever possible, try and encourage them to continue to be themselves with you.

## A Bible passage to consider

Jesus said to him, 'You shall love the Lord your God with all your heart, and with all your soul, and with all your mind.' This is the greatest and first commandment. And a second is like it: 'You shall love your neighbour as yourself.' (Matthew 22.37–39) [See RB 4.1]

## Prayer

May the image of
my maker
in me
and in others
be divine
amongst
the distorted images
of this world.

# 4

## *The love of simplicity*

In my experience, those who have appeared to be most content with life have usually been those who have had the least of this world's material possessions. I can recall when working in a parish in the Midlands how one man's joy was to pack up his fishing gear, leave his house on a local authority estate and walk across some fields to the canal nearby. There he would set up his seat and a small open-sided tent in which he kept his sleeping bag. His flask of hot tea and a large box full of sandwiches would be placed strategically within arm's reach. Having set up his rod and line, and lit his hurricane lamp, he would settle down for a night's fishing. He had everything. He could not have been happier. There was nothing extravagant about his pastime or his lifestyle as his income was less than that of most people. Yet in speaking to him about his all-night vigil and the day's fishing that followed, you would quickly gain the impression that you could not have found a more enthusiastic or peaceful person. Sitting on the bank of the canal having 'set up camp' he was at one with himself, the world and the universe. The father of Roy Castle, the musician and entertainer, once told his son that if he was content with what he had, he was a millionaire. If you are content to this degree, you cannot ask for more; you don't desire more. Indeed, my fisherman friend did not need to go to the Maldives to have the time of his life. He had found it across the fields within easy walking distance of his home.

While twenty-four hours' coarse fishing is not everyone's idea of a good time and not all fishermen are able to live within easy reach of a canal, lake or river, the point here is that it is possible to be deeply at peace with oneself and with the world by engaging in the simplest of activities. The peace of God that kisses the soul with a divine love that brings it to life, cannot be bought or sold. It is available to anyone who with a calm mind and heart is prepared to look deeper into the pools of the Spirit that are formed by the streams of life that constantly surface all around us. Sometimes we try very hard to experience this by spending vast sums of money in the pursuit of the one experience that will make all the difference or the guru that will finally unlock the truth for us. We often fail to see that the truth is not so much out there or over there but within us here where we are.

Running parallel to this is our desire for success or at least the desire to survive by making a recognized contribution that comes with a pension scheme that will keep us warm and at least reasonably well fed to the end. Any number of external *loci of evaluation* compete with each other in this pursuit of security. These can vary from our values and personal understanding inherited from our parents, to living up to the expectations of employers, money lenders or even our spouses and children. In this frenetic scramble to make sure we are among the fittest who survive, we cannot reasonably expect that it might be easy or straightforward to discover the truth. Something has to give. One of the Desert Fathers advises us to 'Cut the desire for many things out of your heart and so prevent your mind being dispersed and your stillness lost.'[1]

Few manage to have both a deep awareness of God and to enjoy the wealth of the world without a commitment to simplicity. But what we mean by simplicity here is not simply the ability to live without a luxurious lifestyle. A life of simplicity is not necessarily one where we only have one coat, one pair of shoes and no dishwasher. Those who have tried to change their lifestyle like this soon find themselves in possession again of the accessories they thought they had given up. The pace at which we have to live today means that we simply do not have time – while holding down at least a part-time job in order to pay the bills – to do the washing by hand and give our children the time and attention we would like to.

So in this sense, to have a love of simplicity is not so much about having few possessions. It has more to do with living without pretence. But the more we surround ourselves with, and rely on, the wealth of this world, the harder it becomes to live simply and unpretentiously. There seems to be something deeply corrupting about wealth. Without our knowledge, we can adopt an inauthentic lifestyle that lacks depth of relationships and connectedness with creation. When we become almost too comfortable in this way, we no longer have to make the effort to live beyond our immediate circle of friends. This in turn can leave us acting out our faith in a way that ignores the demands of love of friends and enemies. Clearly, not everyone who has wealth is prone to this kind of self-deception and there are many wealthy people who are godly and deeply loving. But it, nevertheless, remains a severe challenge to hold on to our soul when we consistently have more than we need. Generally speaking, those with the least are likely to live with little pretence. They have few airs and graces and no need to pretend that life is anything other than it is.

This was the secret of my fisherman friend. While he possessed very little, he had found an authenticity in the simple honesty of his enjoyment of life. He had long ago given up any desire to fulfil the dreams of others. Instead he had found the love that allowed him to be himself. This love does not depend on someone else's opinion of us. Nor do we have to earn it by amassing a high score for good conduct, like tokens off cereal packets. This love comes from deep within ourselves, welling up in our hearts as it seeks to flood our souls, our lives and our loves with the love of God. All we have to do is decide to let it out though many are either afraid of what will happen or are unable to do this until they have rolled away the stone – usually made up of some profound sense of pain, grief or disbelief about oneself – that keeps their love entombed. The *locus of evaluation* here comes solely from God. But not from a God who is like an overbearing parent, nor one who lives so far above the world that he is distant and semi-detached. Instead he is found within each human being, deep within the eternal essence of our selves. While we may experience the existence of God in creation and the universe, he is found and met within the heart that seeks to beat in time with his. And it is our calling that we should so fill our lives with love and prayer that we become increasingly united with God, who alone can bring us to our senses and bless us with the presence of his Spirit. So our divine destiny is guided by the *locus of evaluation* that is to be found within us all. We no longer see ourselves through the eyes of others, the world or even ourselves but through the eyes of God. 'When God looks at a person, He does not see either virtue, which may not exist, or success, which may not have been achieved, but He sees the unshakeable, shining beauty of His own image.'[2]

Here we find the integrity to be ourselves in our own right. We no longer have to define our status by our own unreasonable expectations or those of others. We can be at peace being ourselves whether as an officer in the Royal Navy, a shop assistant, mechanic, company director, university lecturer, nurse, bricklayer or even a priest. In fact, wherever we find this degree of self-acceptance we glimpse the image of God. Then, having recognized it for what it is, we strive to bring it to completion by faith and love. So sitting still by streams of water fishing, or faithfully going to church on a Sunday may be the start but not the end of this wonderful adventure of the soul – where 'deep calls to deep'[3] – that lasts as long as there is breath in our bodies.

> You are sent here to learn to love and to receive love. The greatest gift new love brings into your life is the awakening to the hidden love within. This makes you independent . . . You become free of the hungry, blistering need with which you continuously reach out to scrape affirmation, respect and

significance for your self from the people and things outside yourself. To be holy is to be home, to be able to rest in the house of belonging that we call the soul.[4]

It is as if humanity, destined in the first place to live in heaven, has fallen to earth and in the process fallen out of love with God. Having rejected his love in the heavenly places, we have been called to learn about Divine love so that at the end of our time on this earth we might return to be with our Creator, and find peace at the last with him.

Perhaps the best way to understand how we can believe in the God who is the ground of our being is to look at the way the identity of 'I am' is used to describe God. In the Hebrew Scriptures we read of the time when Moses had an encounter with God that changed his life. A Hebrew by birth but Egyptian by upbringing, he had been forced to flee from Egypt after he had killed an Egyptian soldier who was beating up one of his own countrymen. Moses was now a shepherd and one day while he was looking after his sheep, an angel of the Lord appeared to him from within a bush that was on fire although it was not consumed by the flames. When God sees that Moses has stopped to look more closely, he tells him that he wants him to lead the Hebrew slaves out of Egypt and Pharaoh's control. Then God reveals his name to Moses as 'I am who I am'. This is the continuous Divine Being at the centre and heart of creation. In Hebrew thought at the time, to know a person's name was also to know his identity. It was the same with God. Here, in a unique event of self-disclosure, God is understood in terms of eternal being.

Much later on, when John is writing his Gospel about Jesus Christ, he uses some concepts and words different from those used by the other three Gospel writers to show that Jesus is God in human form. One of the devices he uses is the 'I am' sayings. So in St John's Gospel we read how Jesus describes his divinity and humanity by saying, 'I am the bread of life' or 'I am the good shepherd' or 'I am the Way, the Truth and the Life' or 'I am the resurrection and the life'. John wants us to make the connection that the 'I am' of Jesus Christ and the 'I am' of the God of Moses are one. But there is also a sense in which anyone who can say 'I am' according to the Spirit of Christ acknowledges that their make-up is a mixture of human and divine natures. We would not claim the fullness of divine and human natures that the world has seen in Jesus Christ. But we understand our identity in terms of our potential for union with God through the interaction of our divine and human natures. When we live in the reality of this love, authentically and without pretence, our love puts us in touch with God while making a difference for good in the history of the redemption of the world.

John tells the story of a man who has been blind from birth where there is a discussion as to whether the cause of his blindness is due to some inherited sin from his parents. This notion is dismissed by Jesus and in writing his Gospel John uses this meeting to reveal an aspect of the divinity of Jesus. John gives Jesus the line, 'As long as I am in the world, I am the light of the world.' In other words, God is here in human form as one who brings light into darkness, who helps human beings see themselves through a godly perspective.[5]

But there is a twist to this story as John relates it. After Jesus heals the man there is a double confusion over identity. On the one hand, people just don't believe that the man born blind can now see. They think it must be someone else who looks very like the man they knew. On the other hand, the religious leaders could not believe that Jesus could be from God. In making the blind man see, Jesus had contravened one of the principal religious laws of the time which prescribed that healing of this kind was banned on Saturdays as the Sabbath was a day of complete dedication to God. Yet others of the religious ruling class felt that only a man of God could perform such a miracle. It all becomes very confused as the religious people, the parents, the neighbours and the man himself all try and work out who is telling the truth. It is an extraordinarily long-winded story and there are many aspects to it. But early on in the discussions about what actually happened and who was involved, John includes a line of enormous significance that is very easy to miss.

In a story about how God restores sight to those who are blind, followed by the absurd reaction of those who think they have spiritual insight when they are in fact unable to see the truth, John hides a message that only those who have their eyes wide open will spot. After he has been healed, the man who has been blind tries to convince everyone of the truth of what has taken place by saying more than once, 'I am the man'. This is after Jesus has said, 'As long as I am in the world, I am the Light of the world.' While commentators do not consider the blind man's saying to be one of the great 'I am' sayings of the Fourth Gospel, the juxtaposition of the 'I am' of the healed man and the 'I am' of Jesus is clearly significant for John. It is as if he is saying to those who can see it, 'Look, while he was in the world, Jesus revealed how God lies at the heart of all life. And when you see it, it is like moving from a life lived in darkness and meaninglessness to a life lived in the light of the love of God. And anyone whose eyes are opened by Jesus to the divine potential within him/herself becomes a man/woman of God; a godly person.' So now that we know the significance of saying 'I am the man' or 'I am the woman' whose sight has been restored by Jesus, we can understand how the love of God can become incarnate in us too, from within. When this happens there will be those who won't believe that we are the same person, while others – often within the religious establishment – may struggle with the expression of our divine identity because it hasn't come from within their ecclesiastical structures. But as I intimated earlier, God is known for revealing himself to those who patiently wait by deep pools of water whether they are in Staffordshire or Galilee, or wherever.

So amid the many competing demands of family, friends and wider society, our final identity, meaning and purpose are to be found in the simplicity of faith in God and ourselves. St Benedict describes discipleship in terms of those who 'no longer live by their own judgement, giving in to their whims and appetites' but rather 'walk according to another's decisions and directions' as part of their monastic discipline. To make his point he applies (RB 5.12–13) the following words that Jesus uses to describe his own purpose to the life of the disciple, 'I have come not to do my own will, but the will of him who sent me' (John 6.38). This is not to suggest a denial of our God-given individuality and personality. There are many who have been put off by these words because they think that living according to the will of God is about having to obey long and sometimes unhelpful lists of rules concerning our conduct. But sometimes in order to know and live by the will of God, we have to stop pretending that our way of life is better. Then instead of finding our lives inhibited by the will of God, we discover a new freedom to be ourselves. For the will of God is first of all that we should become the people he has called us to be. Living by his will does not demand our assent to a legal contract. It means instead that we decide to find out how we can fulfil our human and divine potential and where we can best work out his purpose for our life. Once we discover this, we find that obedience to the will of God as we now understand it, is the way to life, freedom and love. It's as simple as that.

\*   \*   \*

## From the Rule of St Benedict

By God's grace I am what I am. (1 Cor. 15.10)

St Benedict uses this verse in the Prologue (RB Prologue 31) to show how St Paul refused to take credit himself for his teaching.

## For reflection

On a piece of paper, write opposite the words 'I AM' as many descriptions as you can think of concerning the person you believe you are. Then spend some time, thinking about where God is in all that you believe you are.

Living without pretence is important if we are to be authentic in our relationships with one another and with God. Are there any ways in which we can become more authentic in the way we live?

## Something to do

Light a candle and sit quietly in a darkened room. Remember the presence of God within you and alongside you in the room. As you look at the flame of the candle, on separate pieces of paper write down the names of any possessions or objects that unnecessarily clutter up your life in the sense that they make it harder to have a simple and honest enjoyment of life. When you have done this, place the pieces of paper into two piles, one consisting of those things you can do something about and the other consisting of those things you cannot change. Resolve to do something with the possessions or objects on the first pile.

## A Bible passage to consider

But by the grace of God I am what I am, and his grace towards me has not been in vain. (1 Corinthians 15.10)

## Prayer

Deep waters of Spirit
flood my heart so full
of your love
that where I am
there you also will be
in me.

# 5

## *The desire for erotic love*

————◆————

Erotic love, like most desires, can be both a source of great depth and stability in relationships and also a great danger and potentially very damaging. In this chapter we shall look at the problematic area of erotic love where at times it is difficult to differentiate between helpful and unhelpful behaviour, turning to a more positive picture in Chapter 6.

Emma (not her real name) was a Christian and an occasional churchgoer. She was in her young middle age, brunette, with gorgeous deep hazel eyes, about five foot six with the body of a twenty-something. She didn't look her age. She had a slightly distant air about her and held her chin up when she talked, giving you the impression that she was looking down on you a little. She wouldn't always look at you when she spoke but, when she did, her eyes held you in a gaze of immense power.

Brought up in the country, as a young girl she had not enjoyed a good relationship with her father. He had been a high-powered business executive and his work left little time for his family. (Emma had one brother.) Unfortunately, the times Emma remembered most keenly from her childhood were times of loss. While she had a loving and generous mother who did all within her power to give her a secure and happy childhood, Emma's self-confidence had been constantly undermined by thoughtless and insensitive comments by her father. It's not as if he beat her or abused her in some horrible manner. He just didn't give her the approval that every daughter seeks from her father. When she passed her exams, she never did quite enough to come up to his exacting standards.

And when she told him she wanted to have ballet lessons, his reply was that it would be a waste of money as she would never be good enough to get to the top. He died when Emma was in her late teens and away at university. And while there was a peace-making at his bedside just before he died, by then, I suppose you could say, the damage had been done.

On leaving university, Emma's life followed a conventional path. She got a job, married, set up home and had two children. The marriage went wrong, she was divorced; if anyone was likely to pick the wrong male partner and end up in an abusive relationship, it was Emma. She had had a number of unfortunate relationships that hurt her deeply, not least because she fell in love many times, allowing herself to become vulnerable to others. And her partners were not always honest or scrupulous with her. Some would say that she was looking for the love her father never gave her. Or, to describe her in a more positive light, you could say that she had a heart full of love, in fact more than enough love to go around. It was as if her background had taught her to value love more highly than anything. Her wounds had given her a Christ-like ability to transcend the institution of the Church with the love that heals. But this had come at a cost.

When asked whether it was altogether wise to give herself to others in the way she had, she could see nothing wrong. As I say, she fell in love easily and while she was not into sleeping around and what might be termed casual sex, she wanted to express her love for her partners in the most physical and tangible way possible. And as far as she was concerned this was by making love to them. And she could see no contradiction between this and her firmly held Christian faith. Why not express your love for someone by becoming naked and vulnerable in complete, intimate self-offering, and why not through your body let them know how much you love them? Although her marriage had gone horribly wrong, surely this didn't mean that she would have to stay forever on her own, lonely and cold in bed at night when she could have the warmth and devotion of another by her side?

Church tradition would frown on such behaviour, if not condemn it. Church teaching is that the proper place for sex is within a stable marriage sanctioned by the Church, blessed by God and witnessed in the local community. But as I say, Emma had done all that and it hadn't worked.

Since very early times, religion has been one of the most cohesive components for an ordered society. The practice of religion may once have been barbaric by our standards but it, nevertheless, will have contributed heavily to the maintenance of law and order. In many cases – not least Christianity – it will have given structure to the establishment of stable family units for the bringing up and nurture of children. Human nature left to its own devices is not attractive, whereas human nature coerced into a moral framework – which may be secular or religious – is more likely to be caring and supportive of all its members. Here its natural instincts are curbed by codes that define individual and corporate moral behaviour, and sanctions are taken against those who decide to opt out. It is frightening at times to see the lawlessness and almost conscience-less instinctual behaviour of those who have lost touch not only with themselves but with what we would call civilized behaviour.

So as far as the organization of stable family units goes, we should be grateful for the traditions of both the Hebrew and Christian religions in terms of the positive effects they have had on the welfare of all, and especially the young and vulnerable. Only now are we beginning to realize the long-term damage done to individuals and society as a result of the decline of the role of religion in society. But, of course, not all religious influence has been for the good of everyone. Some of it has been quite damaging as religious laws from long ago have been applied blindly and indiscriminately to current situations. There are still those who think that the penalties for gross sexual misconduct in the book of Leviticus that date back to a time of religious consolidation hundreds of years before Christ are not wholly out of place. These condemn such behaviour as a man having sex with his mother (penalty death), gay sex (penalty death), sexual relations with animals by men or women (penalty death) and so on. What we need to remember about these laws is that they were devised for a specific cultural situation, as were moral precepts in the times of the New Testament. So, for example, when the tribes of Israel were beginning to establish themselves in the Promised Land among unfriendly and sometimes warlike neighbours, it was important that the birth rate of healthy children was as high as possible. Similarly, while his teaching on divorce is less than clear, you would not be surprised if Jesus did not approve of divorce at a time when there was no legal provision for a divorced woman to have access to housing or income from her former husband and had only the goodwill of relatives to fall back on.[1]

Emma believed that when she thought of her own sexuality in terms of her Christian faith, she could safely ignore all guilt-laden prohibitions that clearly belonged to an earlier age. As far as she was concerned, these were shaped by the needs of people for whom the security and future welfare of the tribe were paramount in an environment of keen competition for land and resources where only the fittest were likely to survive. What is more, she lived in a society in which, since the introduction of the contraceptive pill in the 1960s, it has been possible to enjoy having sex with someone you love – and even with someone you don't but just fancy for the time being – without the fear of pregnancy. So sex in most people's eyes is no longer confined to the purposes of procreation and they are becoming more honest about the way loving relationships are not limited to heterosexuals. Sex before marriage no longer carries the stigma it once had. Today, the vast majority of couples who get married have set up home or at least lived together for some time first. Very few leave their parents' home on the day of their wedding. They've left long before and lived a life of wider personal experience than most of their parents – certainly their grandparents – as they have moved from university to first and second jobs around the country, if not the world. In fact, some relationship counsellors positively encourage an active sex life before settling down, so that the sex life of a couple once they are married – or have entered a lifelong partnership and become completely committed to one another – might be as fulfilling as possible.

So while Emma was the kind of person whose desire for erotic love is very much a part of her make-up and intrinsic to her committed relations with men, she was very much freer than her predecessors to enjoy this side of her life. Until, that is, she fell in love with a man – or woman – who was already in a committed partnership, maybe even married. What happened then when the traditional inhibitors of sexual behaviour had gone? How could she apply the brakes to her desire for love and making love? Or, we might ask, how does any man or woman who is in a committed partnership or who is married apply the brakes when erotic desire – traditionally referred to as lust – arises as a result of biological drives or a cooling of the relationship at home?

It is only in recent years that most of us have woken up to the fact that a very considerable part of our behaviour – some would say most of it – is biologically driven. The reason why religious codes were so important to primitive cultures, and are to some societies today, is that they produce the most ordered environment for mate selection and retention. There is a list at the front of the Church of England's Book of Common Prayer (dating back to the seventeenth century but still in use today) of those it is unlawful for us to marry. Mixing our genes with most of these would be disastrous, for many different reasons.

The two strongest biological survival drives in human beings are those for food and reproduction. The same is true of most mammals and animals and indeed plants and micro-organisms. We all have to – or want to – survive whether by conscious decision or biological programming or both. The alternative is species extinction. In so-called civilized society we can see the same laws that governed the behaviour of our ancestors in the hunter–gatherer tribes thousands of years ago applied in modern hi-tech cities. While it is by no means always the case, I am amazed that we are surprised when a strong alpha male with wide responsibilities in business, commerce, politics, sport or even the Church has a high-profile affair or his marriage breaks down. It stands to reason that males with a lot more than their share of testosterone are likely to have a much greater struggle to remain faithful to their partners than those who have less. One of the dangers here, however, is that erotic desire replaces love, and women are treated as less than human beings worthy of respect, care and love and more as sex machines to be purchased for personal gratification. I dare say there are times when sex for the sake of it both for men and women can be a healthy emotional release for the participants. But women like Emma can very quickly become victims of baser instincts and lawlessness in society.

So it is not good enough simply to argue that in the absence of religious prohibitions, the right to find and express our love in a reasonably uninhibited manner is going to be good in all circumstances. The problem in a way is not so much that Emma was deprived of the love she needed when she was young but that, later on, she had too much love to give. Most people have the capacity to fall in love with more than one person in their lifetime but when you couple this with a deep need that does not fit happily into a conventional partnership, there is scope both for joy and fulfilment and also for sadness and disaster. Erotic love can bring meaning and comfort but it can also be divisive and destructive. Reading between the lines of the Rule of St Benedict, one can see that erotic love between males was considered to be something to be guarded against. 'The monks are to sleep in separate beds. . . . If possible, all are to sleep in one place, but should the size of the community preclude this, they will sleep in groups of ten or twenty under the watchful care of seniors' (RB 22.1, 3–4). Chapter 11 of the Rule of the Master warns specifically about the dangers of homosexual erotic love. We presume that this was for what were at the time considered to be good religious reasons as I have mentioned above and also because such behaviour could be divisive in a relatively small and close-knit community.

Understandably, the reaction of the Church to our desire for erotic sex has generally been to codify what is acceptable and unacceptable behaviour based upon due consideration of biblical texts, tradition and reason. The trouble with this today is that there are wide and different opinions as to how each of these should be regarded and interpreted. The promotion in the Church of gay rights has become the focus for those who hold differing and what appear to be irreconcilable views about these matters. As far as the Church is concerned, it appears that the only way these issues can be resolved will be by skilful diplomacy and political manoeuvring. While all this takes place, wider society looks on and for the most part cannot understand what all the fuss is about. Those outside the institution could be forgiven for thinking that if the Truth that the Church is supposed to embody is as fragile as this then why waste time preserving it in its present form? Fed up with the biblical text message that the Church puts out in order to offer some kind of ordered structure to society and a stable environment for families and most important of all children, others prefer instead to talk not primarily in terms of legal prohibition but of love, its opportunities, demands, its untidiness and its joys – for this is the stuff of redemption.

Emma was a wonderful, loving person and it is very unlikely that she would ever have changed. She discovered God as the ground of her life; she was in touch with him as much as he was in touch with her. And from this place of crucified love she sought to make the most of her life. Maybe she hoped that, one day, the right person would come along who would set her free from her inner yearning. And while some are released from their craving by the love of another, and experience resurrection in this life, for many others and for any number of reasons this does not always happen. They take their cross to the grave, their resurrection is for later.

But we cannot write Emma off because of these deep desires any more than we can write off any man whose particular desire for erotic love imprisons him in a meaningless relationship and sterile marriage. While the gospel is meant to set us free from these things, not all of us escape. But the Christian faith is not only for those who are able to make miraculous changes to their lives and lifestyles, it is also for those who are trapped by unhelpful desires. While the Spirit of creative love offers a better way of life than enslavement to our natural desires, many find the battle between our human and divine natures lasts a lifetime. Few of us – and this includes even the most holy and faithful – are not at some stage or other imprisoned by something or somebody. So it would make no sense to condemn Emma for failing to live up to some unattainable ideal of perfection quarried mistakenly from Holy Scripture. It would have made more sense to help her discover for herself an understanding of the love of God that meets her in her need and remains with her for as long as necessary.

There is a story in the Gospel of John of a meeting between Jesus and a Samaritan woman at a well.[2] Given what we said in the last chapter concerning the significance of deep water, this is a tale full of meaning for those who are in the process of finding God and know that their lives are full of mistakes and good intentions gone wrong.

Tired out by a journey, Jesus stops at a well close by a city called Sychar in the region of Samaria. The disciples go off in search of food, and a Samaritan woman comes to draw water from the well. Jesus has no bucket and the well is deep so he asks the woman to give him a drink. She is taken completely by surprise. Jews did not mix with Samaritans if they could help it. In fact, the Jews despised them. This was because at an earlier date, following the fall of Samaria to the Assyrians, the people living there inter-married with settlers from other countries. Other members of the Jewish nation who stuck to the traditions of their faith (which prohibited marriage to foreigners) felt this was a betrayal of their religion, nation and their relationship with God. And while some remained in Samaria, many others were deported by their invaders and never saw their homeland again. When the ancestors of these exiles did eventually return many years later, they would have nothing to do with those who were descended from those who had done deals with the enemy for their own benefit. They reviled those who had married and had children with foreigners and had diluted the purity of the Jewish nation. They were traitors to their country, and blasphemers before their God. In short they were scum. They weren't regarded as Jews any more. They were Samaritans and bore the kind of name you spat out in disgust. You could pass by their cities, eat their food if you were in need, but you never considered them equal to yourself.

So no wonder the Samaritan woman at the well is surprised when Jesus speaks to her. Jesus tells her that he knows the source of living water that quenches the thirsty soul for ever. This she wants, although she doesn't completely understand just yet what Jesus means. She thinks he is referring to the water in the well. It is time for Jesus to explain further. So he asks her to go and fetch her husband. She replies that she has no husband. Jesus says, 'You are right in saying, "I have no husband", for you have had five husbands, and the one you have now is not your husband.' The woman agrees this is true and presumes Jesus to be a prophet.[3]

This looks like relationship chaos. This woman lived and loved more than most. This woman at the well keeps falling in love but struggles to find a relationship that will redeem her. And in this sense, she represents those like Emma who, try though they might, struggle to make sense of the love they crave and want to give. Maybe she cannot break a cycle of abuse. Maybe she is constantly trying to find the father she lost when she was a little girl. Maybe she likes to sleep around or maybe erotic love has become a tonic for her pain. Maybe she just loves sex and sharing her love with others. The important thing to note here is that whatever she is up to, Jesus does not condemn her. Instead he is gentle with her and leads her to a deeper understanding of Divine love. The Jews and Samaritans worship God on different hills and in different temples. But Jesus says, who gives a damn concerning which hill you worship God on or which Temple you use? Look beyond the religious hypocrisy that surrounds you and understand that what counts when you are with God is whether there is spirit and truth in your heart.

The story continues and the woman comes to understand the spirit and truth in Jesus. She tells her friends that even though God knows the frailty and faith of her human nature, he does not condemn her. Instead, he loves her. Constantly condemned by others' gods for their erotic love of foreigners, the Samaritans are thirsty to hear more. They invite him to their homes, so Jesus stays in the Samaritan village for a couple of days. They end up believing in him themselves because they see in him a love that can save the world.

This is a story of hope for everyone – men and women – whose desire for love has left them vulnerable or confused. It is for those for whom love has gone wrong, for those who have mistaken erotic love for heartfelt love. It is for those who have given themselves completely, in self-giving and self-denying ways to bring pleasure to others and have been left feeling betrayed, exhausted and abused. And it is for those who have been blessed with almost too much love to fit into neat descriptions of so-called 'normal' relationships drawn up by others who themselves frequently give the impression they know very little about love at all.

\* \* \*

## *From the Rule of St Benedict*

With his good gifts which are in us, we must obey him at all times that he may never become the angry father who disinherits his sons. (RB Prologue 6)

Benedict is warning his monks of the need to be faithful to Christ. We have already seen that obedience for the Christian can be understood in terms of our need 'to listen attentively' to God throughout our lives. So while we are concerned first and foremost with love, we need to pursue the purposes of love with great care and in the Spirit of Christ.

# *For reflection*

Take time to read and think about how the following may give you new insight into the nature of faith:

NONINSTRUCTION

'What does your master teach?' asked a visitor.

'Nothing,' said the disciple.

'Then why does he give discourses?'

'He only points the way – he teaches nothing.'

The visitor couldn't make sense out of this, so the disciple made it clearer: 'If the Master were to teach, we would make beliefs out of his teachings. The Master is not concerned with what we believe – only with what we see.'[4]

## Something to do

We can be quick to judge ourselves and others when we or they become trapped by unhelpful desires. Try and think of ways in which you can further understand the actions of those who are caught up in some kind of relationship chaos. It may help to have more faith in them than you do at present.

If you have difficulty in giving or receiving love and maybe feel vulnerable and confused at times, try and find someone you can talk to about this who you think will be able to help you.

If you are fortunate enough to live in a loving relationship, take time to celebrate this with your partner or spouse. Remember to cherish the freedom you have to be yourself because of the faith someone else has placed in you.

## A Bible passage to consider

Come to me, all you that are weary and are carrying heavy burdens, and I will give you rest. (Matthew 11.28)

**Prayer**

Dear Christ of redeeming love
touch me
heal me
embrace me
enfold me in your arms
and make me whole.

# 6

## *The love of wholeness*

———◆◆◆———

In this chapter we look at how we might further understand the love that helps us to make sense of ourselves and how that affects our understanding of erotic love in terms of gift and grace.

While some think that those who are interested in Body, Mind and Spirit are largely found in New Age or alternative spirituality, the aim of the Christian life has always been to strive for wholeness in body, mind and spirit. This is achieved by developing our understanding of how our human nature and the Divine nature can combine to draw us into a deeper understanding of ourselves and God. We believe that we are born into 'a world gone wrong', where good and evil are so intertwined it can be very difficult at times to tell one from the other. In fact, our experience of love rarely comes without also an experience of suffering in a world where pain and suffering form the seedbed of faith as much as – some would say more than – joy and celebration. Ours is a world full of contrasts and apparent contradictions of any creative word spoken by a God of love. Here we see beauty and grace flourishing in times when love is good. At the same time we are aware that this can also be a brutal and callous environment in which to fall in love. For great joy and fulfilment can randomly, it would seem, turn to grief and pain not least in the lives of the innocent. We live in a world where little is assured, where we can only live in the present and where none of us knows what will happen tomorrow, or even later on today.

Among these extraordinary highs and lows of human experience, we are caught up in a love for life, an energy for creation and recreation, that most of us want to hold on to and enjoy. In fact we treasure so much the love that makes sense of our lives that when we find it we want to hold on and preserve it for ever. But if we are to preserve the love that enables us to understand our divine potential and leads us to God, we have to clear away the weeds that can so easily grow around and eventually crowd out our love. For when divine love surfaces in a world where evil also competes for our attention, we need constantly to promote the causes of Divine love at the expense of evil. So when we read the Gospels we find that we are advised that anyone who wants to preserve their life as it is and at all costs is likely to lose it. And on the other hand, anyone who is prepared to lose their life because of the message of Jesus will save it. So we are reminded that we can't have it both ways. If we try to grow in the divine love that makes sense of our lives, we cannot also hedge our bets by investing in materialism. For it is possible to think you have gained the whole world but at the same time to have lost yourself completely.[1] So when, for example, we depend for our security on power, position or wealth, we are likely to miss out on the greater life that we have been called to share. It's not that we cannot have power, position or wealth and be fulfilled in a Christ-like way but that we cannot depend on these things rather than on God. But what does it mean today to depend on God?

One way to depend on God is to assume that he will reward us with material wealth and security. Here faith is not so much about how we bring love and pain together in a creative way but about gross self-interest. While Jesus made it clear that God doesn't work like this, there have always been Christians who think that worldly prosperity is a sign of God's approval. Those who depend on their wealth in this manner, condemn those who, for very good reasons beyond their control, struggle daily to find adequate food and shelter. It also means that those who choose to thrust their faithless hands into a 'pick-and-mix' culture of Christian spirituality can ignore Jesus' more uncomfortable sayings such as 'Take up your cross and follow me', to which we shall return later.

Another way to depend on God is to think that his principal purpose in life is to miraculously alleviate our suffering, from stomach ache to cancer. This is a reasonable and logical position to adopt if we believe in an all-powerful God of love, sense that we are born with a zest for life and believe that he is on our side. But even a superficial reading of the Gospels reveals that when we speak of the love of God, we are talking about a love that becomes most apparent when we stand at the foot of the cross. Here we have to take evil seriously – together with all that disfigures the divine potential of human life – while the love that lies in the heart of God seeks to win through wherever it can. Here our dependence upon God is defined by our ability to find him in all things. And in taking even the most basic elements of life and discovering how they can lead us to God, we uncover the opportunities we have for participating in the Divine energies of creation. As we develop our self-awareness and move from childhood to adulthood, we can change from child-like dependence on God to fulfil the purpose of our lives in companionship with him. We can see how this happens through something as simple yet deeply sacramental as a piece of bread.

When we are very young we are blessed with abundant enthusiasm and energy. Every day is for the taking; to be lived to the full. Every waking moment is filled with exploration, and a seeking after knowledge. The brain's hard drive is thirsty for knowhow to add to the bank of inherited instinctual behaviour. From the earliest moments, we are programmed to feed in order to survive. We begin with milk and we cry and scream if we are not fed on time; though inarticulate, we let our parents know that we expect to be fed so that we can live. As time goes on we learn to feed ourselves, bits of bread or buttered toast are placed in front of us and we are happy to use our gums and what teeth we might have to gnaw away at these tasty morsels. And when we have had enough we cannot yet appreciate that throwing our food across the kitchen is not a good idea, not least because it is wasteful. Some time later we come to realize that we are very fortunate to have the food we need while others grow hungry. And as we share our daily bread with others we come to know that by doing so we are meeting someone else's need while discovering a healing love that can alter the life of humanity for good. Then, through all of this, if we are fortunate enough, we can reach a point of faith that teaches us that eating and drinking in communion with others can become symbolic of God's presence in the world and in ourselves. For here bread and wine symbolize the life and sacrificial love of Jesus Christ. They remind us that as Jesus took, broke and blessed bread, so lives that are taken, broken and blessed by God can reveal Christ's presence to the world.

For today we are re-discovering the understanding that to depend upon God we have first to learn how to depend on our-selves. We have to have a realistic understanding of human nature if we are going to understand anything worthwhile about faith. It is by learning to have faith in ourselves that we learn to have faith in God. Here we discover that the divinity in which we are called to share is the one that is not superimposed from outside as if from the sky. Instead it comes through our inner transformation where, to find the love of God, we have to learn to let go of our ideas of an interventionist God together with our likes and dis-likes, our pains and phobias, our fears and even at times our faith. For the way to God and to wholeness of body, mind and spirit is primarily found in the inner way, the route we take into the depths of our hearts and souls rather than some imaginary and symbolic route to the stars.

We encounter this desire to be whole through what the early Church often referred to as our natural passions. Today we might refer to them as instincts. As we have seen, two of the strongest instincts are to secure food and to reproduce, for they are both fundamental to our survival. If we lived in a world that hadn't gone wrong, we could imagine that they would be more easily controlled. However, in the world as it is, we are only too well aware that while our instincts towards self-preservation keep us alive – together with those around us whom we love – they also need careful handling.

For we can easily eat too much, more than is good for us and for others in the world. And when our eating becomes an end and source of gratification in itself way beyond what we need to survive, we can abuse the love that has given us the resources we are happy to squander. Here as much as anywhere, we need to learn how to depend upon ourselves so that our divinity – our energies for love and life – can defeat our dependence upon the more demonic aspects of our personalities. These demons surface in our desire to have more than we need at the expense of others for, 'If the soul doesn't have a good mind and good conduct it is blind and doesn't know God the Creator and Benefactor of all.'[2]

So while they are not necessarily evil in themselves, we need to understand and control our passions. For through them we can recognize and release the Divine self-giving love of creation. The process of deification of the self takes place when we harness and direct our passions in a godly pursuit of life so that 'The natural passions become good in those who struggle when, wisely unfastening them from the things of the flesh, [they] use them to gain heavenly things.'[3] If the passions remain uncontrolled and unrefined, they very quickly become just another part of our self-interest that we hang on to without any sense of responsibility to others and creation.

One of the greatest stumbling blocks to our progress towards wholeness is that we often tend to take more than we need. And, at the expense of others, we make a god of pleasure. Personal pleasure then becomes the yardstick by which we judge what is right or wrong rather than working out the place our passions should have within the redemption of the world. If it makes me feel good then it must be all right. If it upsets me, it must be bad for me. And this is as true of our experience of erotic love as it is of our squandering of the earth's resources. For here a natural passion or instinct – the need to eat or reproduce in order to survive – becomes unnaturally distorted, demonic even, when we depend on it in a spirit of self-indulgence. Here again we can end up taking more than we really need.

In our practice of erotic love we can see how some of our most basic instincts are challenged by our need to depend upon our divinity. Here the Spirit of love confronts evolutionary necessity where basic instincts are transformed by the unconditional love that comes from God and unites us with him as we express that love in tenderness, generosity and devotion towards someone to whom we have committed our lives. So in our yearning to love and be loved, desire for sexual gratification and to reproduce is confronted by love of another. Self-indulgence is opposed by the Spirit of self-giving love. Here possibly more than anywhere, as we learn the sometimes painful lessons of love, human beings come face to face with the sacramental nature of life. To try to make sense of this sacrament is to know that through a divine perspective we can see – albeit darkly – the potential for Divine love in all human relationships. And as we let go of our lusts for self-gratification which can run riot with our relationships, we begin to release the love of God into the world. So the fusion of two bodies in passionate embrace not only gives physical expression to the love of wholeness, it releases at the same time the Divine love of creation and recreation, if only we could recognize and cherish it as such. Here, possibly more than anywhere else, God comes to life in us. St John writes, 'God is love, and those who abide in love abide in God, and God abides in them.'[4] For when we fall in love we begin to love one another as God loves us. We begin to look at one another through the eyes of God. But this gift of God for the wholeness of humanity has to be handled with love and grace. As we saw in the previous chapter, there are times when we can love almost too much.

The traditional marriage service of the Church of England, which dates back to the seventeenth century, describes one of the reasons for marriage as being 'a remedy against sin, and to avoid fornication; that such persons as have not the gift of continency might marry, and keep themselves undefiled members of Christ's body'.[5] In other words, getting married was meant to stop you sleeping around. In the most recent Marriage Service there is an altogether more enlightened view of the place of erotic love in marriage. Here we read that 'it is given that with delight and tenderness they [the bride and groom] may know each other in love, and, through the joy of their bodily union, may strengthen the union of their hearts and lives'.[6] So while our natural passions may help us regard erotic love as an end in itself, for example as an emotional release or to secure the birth of offspring, by the purification of these passions we find the way to a prayerful union with our partners and therefore with God. For here, instead of merely preserving our genes or ancestry, we come to appreciate our role as co-creators with him of new life and love where we are held in the passionate and intimate embrace of Divine love.

As we slip sometimes unwittingly into a Divine embrace of human and divine spirits, our sexual relations become the unlikely context for holiness when they are nurtured and blessed in faithful and unconditional love of one for another. Here the very act of making love itself becomes an act of prayerful union with the depths of divinity of the one we love whose life lies – like ours – in the heart of God. Here in this dialogue of spirits amongst all the beauty and brutality of life, flowers the life of God, and so we honour and cherish it with all our might as others have done before us:

> Set me as a seal upon your heart,
>   as a seal upon your arm;
> for love is strong as death,
>   passion fierce as the grave.
> Its flashes are flashes of fire,
>   a raging flame.
> Many waters cannot quench love,
>   neither can floods drown it.
> If one offered for love
>   all the wealth of one's house,
>   it would be utterly scorned.[7]

By contrast, when we love selfishly without proper regard for our partners, or ruthlessly for our own gratification, disregarding the sanctity of the other, or when we love deceitfully, taking more than we need, discarding others along the way, we deny our own divinity and theirs. We create a hell of self-obsession and even drag others into it by our madness. Moreover, we desecrate the temple of the Holy Spirit that is the body, and we destroy our – and sometimes their – latent divinity. So high are these stakes that only the heightened self-awareness involved in such acts as confession, forgiveness and reconciliation can redeem us and set us on the right path once again.

So, in order to fully participate in the sacramental possibilities that surround us, we need to live a prayerful life. Our thinking about prayer is often confined to set prayers and times of prayer either on our own or with others. But while it is important to have set times in our lives when we allow ourselves to be more spiritually centred than our busy lives usually allow us, we need also to understand that in a sacramental universe prayer is this and so much more. Therefore, we need both to be disciplined and a bit formal about our spiritual lives and at the same time we need to allow our spirits to be free in their experience and expression of the love of God in ourselves and in one another. In his Rule, St Benedict places great importance on the set times of prayer and on how these are organized and conducted. This takes the form of seven set times of prayer throughout the day. In fact, for Benedict the greatest work we undertake for God is the work of prayer:

> On hearing the signal for an hour of the divine office, the monk will immediately set aside what he has in hand and go with utmost speed, yet with gravity and without giving occasion for frivolity. Indeed, nothing is to be preferred to the Work of God. (RB 43.1–3)

This comes above everything else. For by making room for God in our busy lives – and both monks and nuns can be extraordinarily busy – we receive the grace to unlock the sacrament of our hearts and lives. 'We believe that the divine presence is everywhere and that in every place the eyes of the Lord are watching the good and the wicked (Prov 15.3). But beyond the least doubt we should believe this to be especially true when we celebrate the divine office' (RB 19.1–2). Then, because we have gone out of our way to make room for God in our lives, we are able to extend the hospitality of God to others. The former informs the latter. This is one of the differences between being a good and a godly person, for the latter is given the insight and power to unlock the creativity of the universe. Faith in this sense is that simple, and yet massively sacramental. And this is not without huge significance in a world that is facing the challenges of global warming, where godly people must work creatively together to save unnecessary suffering in creation, and human beings, again by letting go of vested interests, to save life and promote love.

Therefore, by making a priority of being with God at certain times of the day at least, we are all the more able to offer hospitality to him in those we meet. So it is that Benedict in connection with receiving guests says that,

> Once a guest has been announced, the superior and the brothers are to meet him with all courtesy and love. First of all they are to pray together and thus be united in peace, but prayer must always precede the kiss of peace because of the delusions of the devil. (RB 53.3–5)

Rather than being confined to religious rites and ceremonies, prayer unlocks the sacrament of the universe, releasing the love of God so that it can confront, refine and redeem our innate passions. While at one level these passions continue to fulfil their function to promote the survival of the species, at other levels they become ways in which we may become passionate about Divine love. Passion then becomes less about our innate drives and feelings and more about suffering and redemptive love. Hence the passion of Christ. Here in this integration of human and divine spirits we find a wholeness of being and we become a holy people, set apart from and yet servants of those who are subject to their ambitions for worldly security.

Emma (whom we met in our previous chapter) throughout her life continued in her desire to love too much and, through her, others came to appreciate that the desire of God is and has always been for intimate communion with his creation. In this sense she blessed God in her love of others as she drew water for him from the well of life. And in another sense she knew in her heart the pain of the passion of God in Christ as creative love is distorted and twisted into unnatural misuse by the abuse and even hatred of others. Few of us get love right for much of the time. But in a way it is not about getting it right but about a way of being at peace with ourselves and our surroundings. For what matters most is not so much our drive to live a flawless existence – or even less flawed this week than last – nor about our achievement of our divine potential. What counts more than anything is our honest and faithful pursuit of love and peace. Here, with dogged determination and prayerful commitment, we pursue the love that unlocks the life of God in the universe.

\* \* \*

## From the Rule of St Benedict

We must know that God regards our purity of heart and tears of compunction, not our many words. Prayer should therefore be short and pure, unless perhaps it is prolonged under the inspiration of divine grace. (RB 20.4–5)

## For reflection

Think about the people with whom you are in touch. How sacramental is that touch in terms of the way it is grounded in love and reveals the presence of God to others?

How many set times of prayerful devotion do you have and how good are you at observing them? Is there some way in which you can improve on this so that your life orientates less around external forces or internal passions and more around offering hospitality to God.

Among the sayings of the Desert Fathers, one of the hermits said, 'No one can see his face reflected in muddy water; so the soul cannot pray to God with contemplation unless it is first cleansed of harmful thoughts.'[8]

## Something to do

Think of ways in which you might offer the hospitality of God to others and set yourself the challenge of putting this into action.

Think of ways in which your prayerful communion with others and with the world extends to everyday conversations and concerns and to the way you regard and relate to creation.

## A Bible passage to consider

I have been crucified with Christ; and it is no longer I who live, but it is Christ who lives in me. (Galatians 2.20)

## Prayer

Spirit of the universe
by the purification of my heart
set free my divine creativity
that through bread and wine
all things may be blessed
in the prayerful communion
of Divine love.

# 7

## The desire for hatred

On 8 October 1985, *Les Misérables* opened at the Barbican Theatre. Twenty-three years later it continues to delight audiences in London and around the world. Based on the novel by the same name written by Victor Hugo, its huge success is due not least to the way in which it speaks powerfully about the human spirit's fight to free itself from oppression. For oppression can come in many different ways, not least through the abuse of political power that results in the denial of fundamental human rights to the poor, whether this is in nineteenth-century France or in Iraq today. We also experience oppression when relationships go wrong. We may lose contact with our parents at a critical time of our lives or we may lose out in love and forfeit the devotion of someone special and feel only half alive. In this sense, *Les Misérables* is a show for all the seasons of the human heart. It also explores the hope which comes through friendship, and the love that brings purpose and meaning to our lives and even – despite the apparent godlessness of our situation – a glimpse of heaven. At the end of the show, this love is expressed in the words of a song that stirs us to think way beyond the mundane:

> Take my hand
> and lead me to salvation.
> Take my love
> for love is everlasting.
> And remember
> the truth that once was spoken

to love another person
is to see the face of God.[1]

These are brave and prophetic words in a story where love is won only in the context of suffering. But for some, such an experience can end in bitterness, a broken spirit and even a desire for revenge against others. In our experience of pain, we can resent the God who made this life through which we have to struggle, with the odds for survival apparently stacked against us.

While there is a strong natural desire within human beings to survive and enjoy life and to secure as many of the resources and good times as we can reasonably have in any one lifetime, there is also within the spirit of human beings a longing that peace and love may flourish for the good of all. So while freedom and justice are regularly and universally perverted for political gain, this evil is counteracted by an even stronger love that encompasses justice in its broadest sense for everyone. A study of the history of the emergence of the love of God in creation reveals increasingly how we can understand the difference between good and evil and what others before us have referred to as angelic and demonic forces. On the one hand, our human nature causes us to react against the presence of others nearby simply because we consider them to be a threat to our survival. On the other hand, we can see how the Spirit of Divine love deep within us seeks to unite us with others so that we can make the most of heaven and earth together.

The saying 'to love another person is to see the face of God' represents a higher understanding of human relationships, which we discover when we are able to rise above our more natural and basic needs. For while innate spiritual insight comes from deep within the human spirit, it has to compete with other more natural desires for superiority over our competitors. Christ calls us to have this kind of creative relationship not only with those whom we love but also with those whom we have every reason to hate.[2] We may protest that we don't have any enemies, nor do we hate

65

anyone. This may well be the case; however, our personal equilibrium is often achieved by our ability to keep others at arm's length. We relate to them on our terms, initiating a kind of pre-emptive strike in pursuit of our desire for justice in which revenge forms a part. We may regard this as a perfectly reasonable way to maintain our own space and integrity. But at times the tension between looking after our own interests and keeping others at a discreet distance can take on demonic qualities.

One way to establish our security when others are competing for the same resources is to convince ourselves that we have a greater right to them than they do. And if we can also be sure that God wants us rather than our competitors to flourish, we have every justification for treating them in any way we like. Jesus' command that we should love our neighbours – let alone our enemies – at this point goes out of the window. Or, to put it another way, our commitment to a life of Christ-like love often goes unchallenged until we feel threatened by others who have a different approach to life and are competing for the same resources. This innate desire to rubbish others is evident in a trivial way as we compete for parking spaces at our local supermarket, but becomes far more significant when different nations fight over natural resources. Demonizing others who get in the way is a natural part of our behaviour.

As soon as others challenge us, we quickly revert to these natural instincts. Those who have a more fundamental approach to religion – preferring pre-Enlightenment authority concerning how we should live – resort to Holy Scriptures and religious texts to provide a rich resource to justify the division of society and nations into friends and enemies, the saved and the damned. These fundamentalists are quick to defend their own position while denying the rights of others. They don't seem to care much about the damage they inflict on the innocent. This has been apparent in recent years in the Church over the gay rights issue and the rights of women in the Church, or simply through a 'holier-than-thou' attitude. To those outside the Church, in society at large, and to many within the Church, it seems completely absurd that we should want to use words written in different cultures and at a different time in the cultural and spiritual evolution of humanity, to argue that the lives of those of a different gender or sexual orientation are less significant than our own. Different parties claim exclusive access to the Truth, yet fail to appreciate that the test of what is true for humanity can be judged by whether or not it sets the human spirit free in any given age and that this may differ from one generation to another.[3]

As Laura Swan reminds us, 'Christianity is a living, emerging, and growing religious movement. Every generation and every culture engages with and interprets the core message and person of Jesus of Nazareth: *We are not stepchildren; we are all born of God!*'[4] Swan does not mean by this that we should be free to hurt or harm ourselves or others in the cause of freedom of self-expression. That would be to ignore the darker side of our desires. But the freedom to be my best self in society with others and to have equal rights and access to the resources that are freely available to others are basic human rights that no religion or political system should deny.

I can remember being encouraged to demonize in particular the people of the Soviet Union, in the days of the Cold War in the 1960s when the democracies of the West stood against the communist states of Eastern Europe. The people of the Soviet bloc were out to get us, were clearly inferior to us and could never be trusted. Their leaders ruled by terror and controlled their people through draconian laws, the restriction of resources and the vagaries of the secret police and security services. There was a military stand-off in which nuclear missiles were aimed at enemies, and it is frightening to know now that nuclear war was seriously contemplated on at least one occasion. At the time, you felt that if war ever broke out, your enemies deserved whatever they got because you had been led to believe that they were demonic. While power-obsessed leaders from any nation may at times be described as being demon-possessed, the longing of the vast majority of good people, when left alone, is to be able to get on with their lives in peace.

Today in the minds of many, the apparent intransigence of fundamentalist Muslims puts them – and, to some, by default all Muslims – into the same category as the monsters that have threatened Western civilization before. Yet while we blithely demonize whole nations, we forget that in the recent past the West has been responsible for drawing artificial lines across many traditional boundaries of the Middle East. The result of this is that we have ourselves created instability and confusion between competing groups and nations while at the same time trying to establish democracy by military intervention. We have created a situation where the identity of others has been lost because we perceive them to be a threat to our well-being and an obstacle to our access to vital resources. Some in the West even legitimize their desire to hate others by saying that we have God on our side. So we end up with the absurd religious caricature of two extremists fighting one another, one of whom is happy to die for his rewards in the afterlife while the other is happy to die to bring in the end time of God's justice. Given our access to weapons of mass destruction, we could be forgiven for thinking that on these grounds alone, all religions should be banned for ever. It is certainly true that all the main religions of the world – even Buddhism, which has in the popular mind the greatest commitment to peace and non-violence – have legitimized this kind of behaviour for religious reasons at some stage or other, and continue to do so today.[5]

The answer is not, however, to abolish all religions but to look for the truth that lies within them that we need to unlock to free ourselves of hatred and our desire to be better and more powerful than our enemies. Different religions represent the emergence of the Spirit of God at different stages, ways and contexts in the spiritual evolution of the human race. As successive generations have increasingly reflected on the nature and purpose of life, there has been a growing awareness of the Divine in creation. This is expressed in different ways in contrasting cultures, some being more developed than others. In this emerging spiritual consciousness, Christians have been called to seek the face of the universal Christ in others and to understand that we cannot separate the way we regard others from the way we regard him. To find Christ in others – and we may encounter him in any number of different ways, as an outcast by birth or death, or crucified, risen or redeemed – is to discover a new way to understand human beings and the power of love that transforms our relationships.

But how do we go about this? First of all we need to recognize Christ in ourselves so that we can recognize the God of us all in others. We do this first of all by taking responsibility for the pain and love in our own lives and for the way these strong forces affect the way we behave with others. Jesus once said, 'Whoever does not carry the cross and follow me cannot be my disciple.'[6] This is a strange saying because it is placed in the Gospel well before the crucifixion. Reading these words now, we tend to assume that Jesus was referring to his own crucifixion. He was speaking about the need for us all to suffer in a similar way as we, too, give our lives willingly so that love can overcome evil. There are those, however, who maintain that Jesus did not expect to be crucified (the Jewish method of execution was stoning) and if this is the case, these words seem even more puzzling. It may be that these words that refer to the cross of Christ were spoken by Jesus following his resurrection and added in later by St Luke when he wrote the Gospel, at the point where he felt they would make most sense. But the words, 'Whoever does not take up the cross' can also be translated literally to mean 'whoever does not take up the cross of him/herself'. This may give us another way to appreciate what is being said here. For just as the cross for the early Church was the place where humanity's love and the pain of God meet, so 'to take up your cross' could also mean that in order to be a follower of Jesus, we need to be prepared to take responsibility for the place within ourselves where our love and the love of God can redeem our pain and his pain in a fallen world. To be a follower of Christ is not about handing over responsibility for our lives to God but about taking greater responsibility for ourselves and the gift of life that we have been given.[7]

So, to find Christ within ourselves is to find where our love and pain can cooperate with his love and pain to bring healing, in particular in our relationships with others. But first we have to identify where it is that our crosses lie. Where do we need to allow Divine love to heal the pain and restlessness of our souls? Where do we need to recognize the pain of creation? Where can we see that we are causing pain to others? Admittedly, we should expect to be driven at times by our desire to keep others in their place and for our pain and fear to prevent us from seeing God in others, for all this is only part and parcel of our genetic and cultural inheritance. But the challenge of the Spirit of the universal Christ is for us to change so that our lives are energized not by an abuse of power but by powerlessness and authentic love. To be committed followers of Christ, therefore, is not to set ourselves up as judge of others – determining who should be saved and who should be damned – but to purify our hearts and minds not least by allowing our negative passions or natural instincts to be redeemed by sacrificial love. When we do this, we can begin to recognize and welcome Christ into our hearts and lives and to honour him in others. And this applies even and especially to our dialogue with those who are very different from ourselves, those who might object to our understanding of Christ while accepting our desire to let the life of God flourish in everyone.

In setting about this task we have to watch out for those external stimuli that are likely to make us behave in an irrational or unenlightened manner. For example, we need to be aware of the effect the awkward neighbour can have on us, and of those things inside us that prompt us towards self-promotion and the denigration of others – such as the self-confidence that turns into an inflated sense of self-importance.

Amma Syncletica, one of the Desert Mothers of the early centuries of the Church, once said,

> We must arm ourselves in every way against the demons. For they attack us from outside, and they also stir us up from within; and the soul is then like a ship when great waves break over it, and at the same time it sinks because the hold is too full. We are just like that: we lose as much by the exterior faults we commit as by the thoughts inside us. So we must watch for the attacks from people that come from outside us, and also repel the interior onslaughts of our thoughts.[8]

Once we have come to terms with our love and pain, the principal way by which we can become Christ-like in our dealings with others is to make room for him in our lives by prayer. But this is not a prayer for ourselves and our personal salvation but for our relationship with him in the world. As we have already seen, this is achieved by organizing set times in the day for prayer and also by having a prayerful approach to daily life so that we are never far from Christ in our thoughts and actions. This does not mean inflicting on ourselves some weighty kind of praying that actually oppresses us rather than sets us free. It is about finding the right balance so that we can subsume our own hearts in the heart of the universal Christ. We often assume that this kind of a life of prayer is the preserve of those who live in religious communities. We assume that they have the time and have made it their priority to pray at set times of the day and often in the night or in the early morning. But my experience of these good people is that they, too, lead very busy lives and that set times of prayer and prayerful devotion even for them are not easily achieved. So all of us have to make a priority of this kind of prayer; it won't just happen by itself. For only then is the Spirit of prayer released to refresh our lives and restore our sight that we may see the face of God.

What differentiates the members of religious communities from ourselves is their corporate discipline to this way of life, whereas the majority of us have only ourselves to rely on for most of the week. If we don't pray, there isn't usually anyone near us who will make us re-connect regularly with our Divine nature in this special way. Yet while we may find it impossible to pray using set services throughout the day to the same extent as the religious do, there are other more straightforward ways to pray regularly, such as, for example, saying a short one- or two-line prayer on the hour every hour. It is important that we do not see this praying as a way of grovelling before God but rather as a way to re-locate Christ in the centre of ourselves by giving ourselves these opportunities for godly reflection. On these occasions, we become increasingly aware of the Spirit of Christ, as we begin to breathe in time with the Divine creative breath in our hearts. Divine love becomes en-fleshed in human beings through this regular prayerful giving of the self, just as the Divine Self gave his life uniquely in the gift of himself in his Son, Jesus Christ.

Benedict in his Rule is very clear that prayer and love are part of each together. If they are not, we are in danger of becoming followers of Christ in name only rather than by a rededicated way of life. One important area of daily life where prayer and love should go together is in the welcome we offer to others. Hospitality is central to the life of the Benedictine community. Here, as elsewhere, we learn how to become responsible for our preconceived ideas about others by encompassing them in prayerful love. So it is that strangers become our friends as our love overcomes our desire to be stronger, better, more powerful, more independent, more godly than they are:

Once a guest has been announced, the superior and the brothers are to meet him with all the courtesy of love. First of all, they are to pray together and thus be united in peace, but prayer must always precede the kiss of peace because of the delusions of the devil. (RB 53.3–5)

Commenting on this passage, Aquinata Böckmann reflects:

> The kiss of peace is the seal of prayer . . . It is the pledge of goodness and love . . . The instruction to become companions in peace, or to enter into communion through the kiss of peace, can be a program for the task of our world: to create reconciliation and understanding, to further harmony and communion among each other and with God, to seek 'what builds up and promotes peace' (Rom 14.19).[9]

I do not think we can underestimate the significance of this for the transformation of our relationships. Moreover, it is not vastly different from the way most people prefer to behave. Yet while it is so simple, it is very difficult to achieve. We underestimate the enormous power of our natural instincts and while championing their survival value, ignore their darker side. We react to pain and love but we often fail to deal with them in the context of our spiritual development. At the heart of the kingdom of God is a change of heart which is sustained in its reorientation by constant prayerful reflection. And it has to be constant otherwise we return to the default position of our fallen desires. The secret of the kingdom is to allow Divine love to set us free from our earth-bound desires – and to go on setting us free – as we become passionate because we engage in suffering love and abundance of life.

\* \* \*

## From the Rule of St Benedict

You are not to act in anger or nurse a grudge. (RB 4.22)

In the monastery every occasion for presumption is to be avoided, and so we decree that no one has the authority to excommunicate or strike any of his brothers unless he has been given this power by the abbot . . . if a brother, without the abbot's command, assumes any power over those older or, even in regard to boys, flares up and treats them un-reasonably, he is to be subjected to the discipline of the rule. (RB 70.1–2, 6)

## *For reflection*

What do I think I am doing when I am praying? Is my focus on fear or love? How can I become more prayerfully reflective in my daily life?

Where do the crosses of my life lie? Where do I need to be more realistic about the pain and love in my life? How do my pain and love relate to the pain and love of God?

Where do I need to see Christ in others? Where do I need to offer hospitality to Christ in order to further promote peace and love?

### Something to do

Based upon your reflection above, decide upon a course of action that arises out of a renewed understanding of your need to pray, your experience of pain and love or your commitment to offer a welcome to Christ in others.

### Bible passages to consider

You have heard that it was said, 'You shall love your neigh-bour and hate your enemy.' But I say to you, Love your enemies and pray for those who persecute you, so that you may be children of your Father in heaven; for he makes his sun rise on the evil and on the good, and sends rain on the righteous and on the unrighteous. (Matthew 5.43–45)

Then they also will answer, 'Lord, when was it that we saw you hungry or thirsty or a stranger or naked or sick or in prison, and did not take care of you?' Then he will answer them, 'Truly I tell you, just as you did not do it to one of the least of these, you did not do it to me.' (Matthew 25.44–45)

## Prayer

As I let go of my darker desires
and learn to bear the cross of myself,
so may I see Christ more clearly in friend and stranger
and prayerfully hold him in my heart.
Amen.

# 8

## *The love of forgiveness*

Living in a vicarage can provide you with all sorts of different opportunities to offer hospitality to those who seek it. In practice, however, this is rarely straightforward and can be fraught with danger. Not everyone who knocks on your door and asks for help has your best interests at heart. Sometimes they do, or they may simply consider you to be someone who is a soft touch for cash. So it is important to try and work out what kind of need is being expressed in these encounters which can be full of meaning, frightening or downright funny.

Once when I was living in a vicarage on my own, a homeless man came to the door and asked – as was his custom – for a cup of tea (two sugars) and a cheese sandwich. Leaving him standing outside, I went to the kitchen to see what cheese I had. I was horrified when I realized that I was out of cheese except for a packet of very expensive French cheese I had been given the day before as a thank you from one of my parishioners. I had planned to save and savour it one slow mouthful at a time one evening when I knew I would be free of distractions. I suppose it was then that what you might refer to as my Christian conscience kicked in. The words of Jesus, 'Freely you have received, so freely give,'[1] came to mind. How could I, who never went without food, clothing or housing, deny this cheese to one who apparently had so little? With a heavy heart (for no saint am I) I made the cup of tea and sliced the stunningly tasty cheese to sit unhappily in between two slices of standard supermarket white bread. I returned to the door and gave Michael his food and drink. Leaving him to eat it in the porch, I closed the door and went back to my desk. No sooner had I sat down than the doorbell rang. I returned to the threshold of my faith and his feast. Opening the door, I was met not with gratitude but with frustrated incomprehension. 'What's this?' said Michael holding the sandwich in obvious distaste in his huge and filthy hand. (He'd only taken one bite out of it.) 'That is very special and expensive cheese, not something you come across often,' I replied with a mixture of enthusiasm and justification. 'You've been 'ad, mate,' said Michael. 'This ain't cheese. I can't eat this muck. Haven't you got any cheddar?' The words, 'Freely you have received, Michael, so freely eat and appreciate, you ungrateful so-and-so,' came to mind as I realized that neither he nor I was going to enjoy this delicacy. But what did it really matter? I wasn't starving and Michael was used to cheddar.

Sometimes, we are given encounters with those whom we think are in need of our help and generosity when in fact it is our need they have been sent to meet. It is so easy to assume that because we have food and financial security, we are the ones who need to help the poor. We don't often think about what they have which we need. After all, what have they to give to us? The uncomfortable answer is sometimes, 'Everything, even our souls.' We just have to have our eyes open enough to recognize the Christ who sometimes blesses us in very unusual ways and through unlikely people.

It was good to meet another homeless man who came our way for the first time recently. I had not met him before and we tried to help him as much as we could. After all, he was a welcome guest. He was gentle and never demanding in his requests. We readily supplied hot water and cups of tea whenever asked. Sleeping accommodation was arranged. And whenever you met him, he always had a smile and a reassuring word for you. But over the weeks, he began to get in the way.

Angus slept in the church porch over the summer months. The deal was that he didn't make a mess, and he kept his word. (After all, what kind of a church are we if we cannot offer some kind of hospitality to those who have no home?) He didn't appear to have any money but ate well from what was thrown out by the restaurants in town. A well-built man, he had a physical presence which for some could be intimidating, particularly when he adopted the churchyard as his garden at awkward and inconvenient times. The last straw, I suppose, was when Angus used the bench by the area set aside for the burial of ashes for sunning himself. It wasn't appropriate, particularly when grieving relatives came to pay their respects near to their loved ones' mortal remains only to see Angus's half-naked body prostrate on the ground, fast asleep in sunbathing pose.

While Angus was nothing but polite and well meaning, he was an untidy and unpredictable presence in a well-ordered and stable environment. We heaved a sigh of relief when he told us he had decided to return home – although while he hadn't actually said as much, we had assumed he didn't have one! He packed his rucksack one last time, came and shook my hand and said goodbye and thanked me for all we had done for him. It was only after he had gone that I realized Angus was not homeless after all. In fact, he had a house in Devon and had finally decided to leave us because his wife had rung him on his mobile to say it was time he went home.

What should we make of this? Some might feel annoyed that he stayed in our churchyard at all. Others might object to his scrounging a free holiday by the sea at our expense and inconvenience. He was strong and fit. Why didn't he have a job to support his wife and maintain his house? Why on earth walk and hitch all this way to the North West of England and eat the scraps that fall from the tables of those who have earned the right to eat out when he could have stayed in his own home? Why sleep in the church porch – although it's a view to die for with views across the churchyard to the sea – when he could have slept at home?

And who is Angus? Is he an irresponsible scrounger who lives like a parasite off others and refuses to own up to his responsibilities at home? Is he a self-made multi-millionaire who from time to time likes to bring himself down to earth and recall what life was like before he made his fortune? Or is he an author researching a book on living in the churchyards of England, a sort of Michelin Guide to churchyard porches and benches and nearby restaurant bins? Or is he an ex-serviceman who, with mind misshapen by action in Iraq and Afghanistan, needs from time to time to get away and wander on his own? With only the clothes he wears to protect him and the contents of his rucksack to comfort him, he searches for the kindness and goodwill of strangers to restore his belief in humanity and maybe even in God.

We do not know the answer to these questions and it is probably none of our business to ask. It is up to Angus to tell us about himself as and when he wants to. All I know is that he came and asked for help and hospitality and we tried our best to respond. He didn't threaten anyone or damage anything but he didn't play by our rules all the time and so became something of a nuisance. Our tolerant natures did not cope well when we saw Angus's smalls laid out on the church wall to dry.

As we have seen, Christians are encouraged to show warm and generous hospitality to strangers and to understand that by doing so they can learn something powerful about themselves and God. 'Do not neglect to show hospitality to strangers, for by doing that some have entertained angels without knowing it,'[2] we are told. In the visible absence of any wings or halo, should we be right to assume that Angus does not fall into this category? For the word 'angel' means 'messenger' so anyone who brings us a message from God might in this sense be called an angel. Then what message, if any, did Angus bring us from God?

St Anthony – often referred to as the founder of monasticism – once said, 'Our life and our death are with our neighbour. If we are to do good to our neighbour, we do good to God; if we cause our neighbours to stumble, we sin against them.'[3] It is a sobering thought that my salvation is not after all about making a private deal with God about my long-term future. If we take St Anthony at his word, our salvation seems to depend not only on how we are with God but also upon how we are with others. In fact, it is a mistake to separate the two. Didn't Jesus say that we should not separate our love of God from the way we are with other people?[4]

Could it really be that we are responsible not only for our own salvation – our life and death – but also the salvation of others? And do they not hold our salvation within their hands, too? We cannot work out our own relationship with God without working it out with those around us. So it is no good saying, 'It's his problem' and leaving it at that. Nor is it any good refusing the help we are sent through others even if they are not our kind of people. To some degree, we need to take 'his' or 'her' problem on ourselves to help them. And where appropriate, we need to let them share our burdens, too. For we are called not only to be reconciled with others when we have a problem with them but also to go to others who have a problem with us and help them sort it out.[5]

So what can I learn from Angus? Well, he has made me think about my relationships and the need to see my faith not simply as something that belongs primarily or exclusively between myself and God. For faith is also about having faith in others, even in the most unlikely circumstances. And while we have had to deal robustly with several other folk who have asked us for hospitality but were both unreasonable and irresponsible from the start, I would like to think that we will always try to help those who are in genuine need.

My abiding memory of Angus is his gratitude for life itself. He had an extraordinary appreciation for the gift of every day and the need to live life one day at a time, wherever possible. His presence in my life for a while also makes me wonder whether daily we are surrounded by 'angels' who are sent to teach us about God and bring about our salvation? If only we could be more aware of them. It seems as if we are given each other's prayerful company in order to fulfil our destiny. For we hold the secret of others' salvation in our hearts and lives as well as our own.

The mark of Cain was a sign for all humanity to remember that we should never take the lives of others – not least those of our relatives – for granted because we think we have more rights than they to life and the favour of God.[6] We need each other too much to make this kind of mistake. The monks who lived in the desert often spoke of the need not to make false assumptions about others: 'Joseph asked Poemen, "Tell me how to become a monk." He said, "If you want to find rest in this life and the next, say at every moment, 'Who am I?' and judge no one." '[7]

So this is but another example of the way in which the love of God is constantly at work on our desire to think of ourselves as superior, more important or better off than others. God works through the insight that love gives us to draw us into the way of Divine love so that we might fulfil our potential to love in a Christ-like way. Some time ago, a great friend of mine wrote to me – as he did to all his close friends – to let me know that he was 'coming out'. In other words, he was letting us know that having kept it quiet for many years, he had come to realize and accept that he was gay. He now wanted everyone to know the truth about himself so that he could be true to us. We thought he was doing us a favour. Others may have thought that he was admitting to a moral or spiritual flaw that they did not have, for this was not a scar that they shared. Some of us were better than that. Overall, we were delighted that he felt he could tell us, for at that time to be gay carried some social stigma with it in a way that is not the case today. Love cannot heal what is hidden away. But it was not my friend who needed healing from his sexual orientation. It was our misunderstanding – even our prejudices – of the significance of his sexuality that needed to be 'outed' in order for us to be healed. Some would say that we needed to forgive him when in fact our need of his forgiveness was far greater.

Forgiveness, rightly understood, sets us free from our natural passions to engage in passionate love for others whereby we become complete by sharing in one another's pain and joys. No one who lives for him or herself alone or who makes a priority of their own survival while remaining unconcerned about the welfare of others can achieve this. In the Prologue to the Rule, St Benedict encourages his monks to run 'with hearts enlarged' the way of faith so that our hearts will overflow 'with the inexpressible delight of love'. And it is vital that we heed this advice if forgiving love is to fill our lives.[8] For the amount we are able to forgive depends upon how open and large our hearts are. Those who respond to threat and pain with forgiving love are often those whose hearts have already become open because of the positive way in which they have responded to love and pain in the past. On the other hand, those who have rejected love and pain and have sought only to protest their innocence through their indignation at the unjustness of life, will find it very difficult to find true forgiveness in their hearts.

Many seem to think of forgiveness primarily in terms of a single act whereby we say, think or pray the words, 'I forgive you.' And when we discover the feelings of pain and resentment are still there despite our prayers and confessions, we condemn ourselves for failing to live up to the teaching of Christ that we should forgive others so that God can forgive us.[9] We therefore send ourselves to hell and lose confidence in the gospel's power to save because it hasn't worked for us. But while forgiveness does include the ability at some stage or other to say to the person or people who have caused us pain, 'I forgive you,' forgiving love is most of all about being in a relationship of grace with others. Here despite our shortcomings, our fears and dislikes, we are held in a relationship of love with others, not so much because we like them but because we are committed to them and their welfare, as together we hold the secret to the welfare of others and the salvation of a whole world of needy people. In our relationship with God, grace holds us close to his heart not because of our goodness, but because of his commitment in terms of his unconditional love for us. In this kind of graceful relationship, while we need at times to say sorry and to forgive, the love that binds us together is such that forgiveness is given almost before the act of defiance – against God or a fellow human being – has been committed. For the priority here is the love and well-being of the other rather than our selfish survival instincts.

Benedict is quite strong in his dealings with those who break the Rule through bad behaviour. Self-discipline, honesty and obedience are highly valued as they keep us from unruly behaviour:

> If someone commits a fault while at any work . . . either by breaking or losing something or failing in any other way in any other place, he must at once come before the abbot and community and of his own accord admit his fault and make satisfaction. If it is made known through another, he is to be subjected to a more severe correction. (RB 46.1–4)

So forgiveness is found in our willingness to have hearts that are open and large enough to cope with the pain of the world that we come across. Forgiveness is found here rather than in saying a formula of words that we think by itself frees us from resentment. But we have to work hard to enlarge our hearts in this way by prayer and love. For only those who are seeking to live by Divine love can forgive in this way.

We cannot go far along this path unless we are prepared to admit our own mistakes. How can I learn from those whom God has led to cross my path, if I am not able to understand my need of them in the first place? If I had no need of them, I would be perfect. In that I am anything but perfect, I have areas in my life where I must own up to myself at least that I am flawed and in need of greater faith. Just as I have faith in God and need to strengthen this faith, I need also to have faith in myself and others and continue to strengthen my faith in myself and them.[10] If I who live in a comfortable vicarage am challenged by some who knock on my door, I probably need to admit that while I eat well, I do not have sufficient regard for those who do not. And while I am supposed to help others find their own salvation, I need to remember how much I have to learn from them. So confession – which for many in the Church is understood in terms of set prayers said daily or on Sundays or at special times of the year – is as much about being honest with oneself as it is about being sorry to God.

For without this honesty, our prayers of confession and absolution are unlikely to set us free to grow in love and grace.

We need to be aware, therefore, of the dangers of claiming a love that we have inherited by following religious law. For this is not real love. The love of Christ only comes to us when we confront ourselves. The doctrines and liturgies of others are meant to help us do this but we can use them as a place of self-justification where we can hide from our passions while pretending to be close to God. Dietrich Bonhoeffer, the German Lutheran pastor and author who was executed by the Nazis in 1945, reminds us of the need to differentiate between cheap and costly grace:

> Cheap grace is the preaching of forgiveness without requiring repentance . . . is grace without discipleship, grace without the cross, grace without Jesus Christ, living and incarnate . . . Costly grace is the gospel which must be *sought* again and again, the gift which must be *asked* for, the door at which a man must *knock* . . . Such grace is *costly* because it calls us to follow, and it is *grace* because it calls us to follow *Jesus Christ*.[11]

Forgiveness like this also requires patience. Not just for those we seek to forgive but also for ourselves as we attempt to deal with the negative passions, or instincts, that divide rather than unite us. While we may feel we should forgive someone who has offended or hurt us, we may find that this takes much longer than we had expected. For it only 'happens' when divine love has reached a point of self-expression in our hearts or souls. Until that moment of grace, our lack of forgiveness, dislike of others and feelings of revenge are held in check by a decision in the mind that we will remain committed to the welfare of others. Some do find they reach a moment of forgiveness – sooner or later – when a relationship is changed for good. Others find their pursuit of forgiving love may last a lifetime. Either way, forgiving love becomes a reality for us either partially – in our honest pursuit of it – or fully in the grace of Divine love.

\* \* \*

## From the Rule of St Benedict

Pray for your enemies out of love for Christ. If you have a dispute with someone, make peace with him before the sun goes down. (RB 4.72–73)

## For reflection

One of the brothers asked Isidore, the priest of Scetis, 'Why are the demons so afraid of you?' He said, 'Ever since I became a monk, I have been trying not to let anger rise as far as my mouth.'[12]

How often have I allowed anger to obstruct my love for others? Who do I need to ask forgiveness for this? While anger is a natural and sometimes right reaction to certain circumstances, how can I best express and also control my anger so that I may use it in the cause of love?

### Something to do

Try and become more aware of the occasions when you are drawn into the company of others maybe even for the first time. As you become more aware, listen attentively to what they have to say as their words may well be intended for you. They may be an answer to a prayer you have said or they may be part of God's prayer for you.

### Bible passages to consider

Therefore we must pay greater attention to what we have heard, so that we do not drift away from it. For if the message declared through angels was valid, and every transgression or disobedience received a just penalty, how can we escape if we neglect so great a salvation? (Hebrews 2.1–3)

Do not neglect to show hospitality to strangers, for by doing that some have entertained angels without knowing it. (Hebrews 13.2)

## Prayer

Lord,
enlarge my heart
and fill it with forgiving love
that by meeting you in others
my salvation and theirs
may be complete
in the grace of your eternal life.

# 9

## *The desire to be in control*

In the West it is very easy to become ignorant of the great wealth we possess and to ignore, or just simply to be unaware of, the effect this can have on the human soul. Many of us struggle with the affluent version of Christianity that predominates in this country; the simplicity of the life of Jesus and his disciples and the complexity of life today bear little resemblance to one another. Occasionally these contrasting cultures clash in our conscience when we consider how few are the lifestyle changes we have made because of our faith. Sometimes, afraid of facing questions concerning the relevance of a two-thousand-year-old faith that originated in the Middle East, we try and tighten our control on our religious resources lest we should lose them altogether. We fail to understand that to loosen our grip on tradition and to allow our theology to speak to the modern mind in terms it can relate to, is not weakness but strength.

Autocratic leaders who exercise an extreme degree of control over their people often resort to armed force to reduce the freedom of others so that they can remain in control. Or they can lay almost exclusive claim to the truth as revealed to them by God, and this – incredible though it seems to most of us in a secular society – can be used even today to start wars. On a lesser scale, where there are despots in business, education and the Church, you find similar fiefdoms where bullying goes unchallenged not least because of an autocrat's control over people's income or chances of preferment. Among family relationships there are many subtle ways that are employed by those who are insecure about their lives and relationships to manipulate others in order to control them.

The type of person you are and your personal history often determine the amount of control you want to achieve. Most of us want some degree of control. Having a house to live in – rented or owned – provides a degree of control. But the more we feel we are into control, the less well we cope with those who are not, and vice versa. Unfortunately for the religious control freaks, Jesus seems to want to set people free – from the control systems of others and from their own need for control of life – so that they might be able to love freely. His demands are often untidy and unpredictable, for we are likely to lose all control when we begin to love our enemies. While some prefer to return to a more disciplined approach to church life, others feel it is time to look for a new way to help humanity believe in itself. The danger with the increasing patterns of control in our lives – from CCTV monitoring of behaviour to satellite navigation where many wrong turns up blind allies are made by drivers in blind obedience to High Tech – is that we are giving ourselves fewer and fewer opportunities to explore and express our freedom to pursue God's purposes.

Jesus once tested the vocation of a wealthy person who wanted to follow him by telling him that first he had to sell everything he had and give it to the poor. We are told that the man was shocked by this for he felt he was pretty good at keeping the religious laws that guided his way of life and kept him in touch with God. But clearly, he could not let go of his wealth. His reaction to Jesus' challenge is understandable and would probably be ours as well. We read 'When he heard this, he was shocked and went away grieving, for he had many possessions.'[1] The point here is not simply that great wealth and strong faith do not easily go together but that the man had not realized how wealthy he was and the effect this could have on his ability to be faithful to Jesus. His wealth was giving him a false sense of control.

I am sure I would have reacted in the same manner as this wealthy man. I have come quite naturally not only to depend upon my material possessions and the comfort they provide but also through them to develop a sense of control over my life. The present becomes more manageable and the future more predictable when we can afford what we want. While those who spend vast sums of money on their children's education are doing what they feel is best for their children's development, some of them will also be buying into a controlled and predictable future for their offspring. The relative security of a good job and income, however, are not always guaranteed and can come at the cost of individual freedom. When children are subjected to too much control of their development, they can assume the values and beliefs of their parents without working out their own views on these matters. They grow up and work hard simply to send their offspring back to the same schools of controlled survival.

So the rich man in particular finds it difficult to give up his wealth not only because he has become used to the comforts of life but also because without them, he would have to rely on others and trust in God much more. By this I am not suggesting that God does not want us either to be responsible about how we live or that our lives should be out of control. Far from it. As we have seen, Love's desire is that we should control our negative passions and instincts and work to get rid of them in favour of our positive passions and instincts. But we have a natural tendency also to want to assume control of our lives and destiny in a way that can give us a distorted understanding of ourselves and of God. Unsurprisingly, when something beyond our control happens to us and we are intimidated or frightened by circumstances and cannot sense God coming immediately to our rescue, we feel hard done by. We mistake our desire to control life for God's desire that we should fall in love with him and forget that the two are in fact incompatible. Love is untidy and unpredictable; as soon as we try to control it, we begin to deny it to some degree or other.

Wealth at the time of Jesus was seen not as a curse but as a blessing from God. There were many who believed that if you lived a good and religious life and avoided committing some heinous crime,

God would look after you, and your business would flourish. Not so, says Jesus. Love asks you to put your faith in others and in God. Yet it is all too easy to construct a way of life by which we become committed to following the teaching of Christ today while being ignorant of the way our desire to control life influences this. Sometimes this desire is so powerful and our ignorance of it so great, we end up with a picture of Jesus Christ that – like the rich man in the story – bears very little resemblance to the reality of God. The greatest human ambition of all is to seduce God into giving us control of the universe. Jesus told a very powerful story about the way God kept sending messengers and even his own Son to show humanity how to live. Tragically, instead of heeding the various messages, the people decided to kill even the Son so that they could then run their lives in the way they wanted without outside interference.[2] So somewhere between inauthentic religion that fails to give expression to authentic faith and the desire to do away with God altogether, we are called to follow the wandering Galilean. He offers a way of life where we are realistic about how much we as created beings belong to the earth and about our divine potential and how ultimately we belong to heaven.

Perhaps the most frightening reaction of all to our desire for control is that of ignorance. If we struggle against God for the ownership of the universe, we are at least admitting we are not the authors of life, although we want to be. But if we don't realize the extent to which we are trying to control life, we have reached a point where we are only really concerned with ourselves.

I once received a postcard from a Christian friend of mine who was always writing to me and others, proclaiming the Christian faith and how much good it could do in the world. Yet when I received a letter from her after a visit to Africa, all she could write and talk about were the beautiful sunsets she had seen. Her blindness was breathtaking. On the one hand, she could write about how God was answering her prayers for good health when she was at home and living a comfortable middle-class existence. On the other hand, she could go to an African state on a continent in crisis and see nothing of the suffering of millions of indigenous black Africans. She seemed to have God completely under control.

This desire to be in control in the sense of assuming power for earth and heaven is often referred to as pride. In the myth about Adam and Eve in the Garden of Eden,[3] it was their pride – their arrogant desire to control the whole of life on their own or even their blissful ignorance of the negativity of this desire – that brought about the big falling out between themselves and God. They thought they could do what they liked and everything would be all right. Unfortunately, individual experience and the history of unredeemed human ambition show them to be wrong. In other words, while God calls us to develop the Divine power within ourselves to promote love and peace, if we insist on pursuing not only the good but also the evil opportunities we are given in life, we are likely to end up living at a distance from God and constantly buffeted by our lust for power. In this sense, pride is the greatest sin of all where sin is understood to be the way in which we fail to fulfil the possibilities of our human relationships and our relationship with God.

As we seek to develop our faith in God, it is natural to assume that we begin by expanding our knowledge of God through the Church, its Scripture, creeds, history, tradition, worship and so on. Unfortunately, a lot of Christian education looks like indoctrination when developing knowledge of the faith is not matched by a similar developing knowledge of oneself. For all this knowledge – and we can spend a lifetime acquiring it – is of little use if we do not at the same time develop our faith in ourselves. And faith here consists of an appreciation of human nature in its evolutionary setting and of our growing awareness of life in terms of the spiritual evolution of humanity. In any close human relationship there are degrees of control at work.

This emphasis on self-awareness might appear to be playing into the hands of human pride and putting our own interests before God. But this is not the case precisely because our aim here is to understand ourselves and our place in this world in relation to

God who is in, through, beneath, above and beyond all things. This is what the pursuit of humility is about. For humility comes from acknowledging our place in creation and learning how to live in reference to that. Or you could say it is about discovering where the Spirit of Christ is in your life and living in communion with him.

The Christian begins with two basic beliefs about human nature. These are that we are made of the earth and also created in the image of God. Humanity, therefore, is fundamentally good rather than basically evil. My earthly frame belongs to this world and it will be returned to the earth when my mortal life comes to an end. But there is another part of me which is described in terms of the Spirit which God breathed into the soul of humanity that seeks to grow in Divine love and belongs to God.[4] So in Christ we are made up of body and Spirit, temporal and eternal, children of God who have been called to make his incarnate love a reality in our lives. We cannot differentiate where earth and heaven meet within ourselves for in this life, as we have already seen, both are inextricably bound together. But when our behaviour reveals the love of God, something of that Spirit is revealed and similarly when our behaviour reveals a false pride that seeks to control our destiny, something of the spiritual disarray in us is revealed. And as Christ becomes the model of this new life, we seek to imitate his humility which grounded him both in this world and in the life of God.

The word 'humble' when applied to human beings means literally to be a lowly person or 'of the earth'. In other words, our commitment to humility refuses us any illusions about our power to control life or God. Humility is the opposite of pride. It means that we are realistic both about our 'earthiness' and also about our divinity. For only when we are humble about our place in the world and our significance in the evolution of humanity, can we begin to live the life of God. It was in the earthiness of a humble birth that Christ was seen to proclaim that 'God is with us'.[5] And the first to kneel before the manger were shepherds, considered at the time to be very lowly individuals indeed, at the edge of respectable society. Yet from the fields, living under the stars, they were led to Christ.

St Benedict writes at some length in his Rule concerning what he describes as the twelve steps of humility. He wants to make clear how important it is for his monks to understand that access to heavenly things comes only through the offering of our humanity in the service of God and others. He introduces his steps of humility by first referring to the story of Jacob's dream at Bethel.

The story of Jacob is about someone who understood his vocation but who at first sought to achieve it by deceit and treachery. During pregnancy, his mother had been told that each of the twins in her womb would be the father of a nation but that the elder would serve the younger. But as the younger of the two sons, Jacob became frustrated because according to tradition it was the elder brother who received the father's blessing and inheritance. So, with his mother's help, Jacob set about taking control of his destiny. He decided he would make his vocation come true by deceit and that, in the process, he would take control of his father and elder brother.

When his trickery came to light, he was forced to flee for his life. His brother Esau was none too pleased to have been cheated out of his inheritance and as a result decided to kill Jacob. Instead of being in control, Jacob suddenly discovers that his life is completely out of control. So it is highly significant that as a refugee from his own home, sleeping rough one night in a desert place, he dreams of a ladder going up to heaven from where he lies, with angels ascending and descending the rungs (Genesis 28.10–22). Here in this state of powerlessness, where selfish human ambition has failed, God gives Jacob back his vocation. 'As he sleeps, Jacob has this extraordinary dream about a ladder. Climbing it was not an option. Instead of promoting his own ascent, Jacob was asked to pay attention to the descent of God into his life.'⁶

This is not an unfamiliar experience for many. Pride often comes before a fall and some of the greatest opportunities we are given to understand the true significance of life come when we are down and out. In *The Ladder of Divine Ascent*, St John, a monk living in the Egyptian desert in the sixth century, describes the twenty-third step on the ladder in the following terms:

> Pride is a denial of God, an invention of the devil, contempt for men. It is the mother of condemnation, the offspring of praise, a sign of barrenness. It is a flight from God's help, the harbinger of madness, the author of downfall . . . It is the denial of compassion, a bitter Pharisee, a cruel judge. It is the foe of God. It is the root of blasphemy.[7]

When our pride has led us to our knees, we can react in any number of different ways. We can become hell bent on climbing back to where we were, we may become embittered by our bad fortune, or we may learn from the experience about what really matters in life. By coming to terms with our humanity, by understanding our earthiness, we discover that humility is vital for the fulfilment of our dream of divinity. So we cannot underestimate the significance of the place where Jacob had his dream. He was in a wilderness and his pillow was a rock. Reduced to lying on the earth alone in this place, his new-found earthiness led him to God. He even named the barren, stony place 'Bethel' meaning 'House of God'.

Benedict goes on to introduce the subject of humility by explaining the steps of humility by which we ascend into the presence of God. But first he describes how we might understand the image of the ladder for our own lives:

> Now the ladder erected is our life on earth, and if we humble our hearts the Lord will raise it to heaven. We may call our body and soul the side of this ladder, into which our divine vocation has fitted the various steps of humility and discipline as we ascend. (RB 7.8–9)

Here our desire to control our lives has been superseded by our service of God in body and soul. The steps of humility are designed so that we may rise above selfish ambition and use our lives as an offering for the long-term good of creation rather than as an investment in short-term, predictable rewards. Thus by adopting this humble way of life, we reach some way beyond the stars.

\* \* \*

## From the Rule of St Benedict

The first step of humility, then, is that a man keeps the *fear of God* always *before his eyes* (Ps 36.1) and never forgets it. (RB 7.10)

## For reflection

Allois also said, 'If you really want to, by the evening of one day you can reach a measure of godliness.'[8]

### Something to do

Take time to sit prayerfully in a dark and deserted place either early in the morning or late at night and imagine the rungs of a ladder stretching up to heaven from where you are sitting. Imagine the rungs are steps of humility you need to take in your ascent to God. Then ask yourself what you think the rungs would represent in your life. What steps of humility do you need to take? As you do this, pray about how you might best climb this ladder.

### A Bible passage to consider

Transgression speaks to the wicked
    deep in their hearts;
there is no fear of God before their eyes.
For they flatter themselves in their own eyes
    that their iniquity cannot be found out and hated.
                                    (Psalm 36.1–2)

## Prayer

God of creative love
keep me down to earth.
Christ of redeeming love
lead me through this life.
Spirit of sanctifying love
raise me up to heaven.
Amen.

# 10

## *The love of letting go*

———••••———

We have a small but striking watercolour painting at home. The foreground is dark and in the centre stands a large stone Celtic cross. It stands silhouetted by the rising sun and the reds and oranges of a dawn in springtime. It was painted in a churchyard in the hills outside Lancaster where we had converted the adjacent vicarage as a retreat centre for those who lived in urban priority areas.[1] On a residential weekend, a group of women whose lives were bound up in very difficult circumstances were encouraged to express themselves through painting. This was a new experience for most of them. And the results were staggering. For under professional supervision and free of constraint, images of great power and beauty emerged quite naturally from hitherto unexpressed depths of spirit. Most of the women had no idea that they could paint, while others hadn't realized the power and eloquence of their feelings once committed in paint to paper. The beauty of the spirit of the woman who painted the picture that now hangs in our house is matched by her extraordinary ability to sense the significance of the Spirit of creation in the beauty that surrounded her very early on that March morning a few years ago. For in the centre of the colours of dawn is the brightest point of light as the radiance of the rising sun projects the lines of the cross almost into the room. Here in that quiet churchyard, free of the dreadful and sometimes demonic desires of others, the Spirit of Christ, the Spirit of the universe, surfaces to stun the spirit of fallen humanity with the beauty of the love of God.

Here humility is not primarily about learning how to serve others. This comes later. In these very early stages, in this dawn of faith, we see in the drawing and painting of those in pain an unexpected glimpse of earth and heaven. Here our earthiness and our divinity combine to produce a new view of life, where darkness gives way to light and new possibilities for love constantly emerge.

Having used the story of Jacob's dream at Bethel as a picture for our ascent into God, as we saw in our last chapter, Benedict goes on to describe the first of twelve steps of humility. The first step, he says, is to acknowledge God's claim on our lives and to live accordingly. For now we are to live not for ourselves alone but for God (RB 7.10). This is precisely what the group of women at the retreat centre had discovered, although they might not have used these exact words. But they had come to realize afresh that it is love that makes most sense of life. We need, therefore, to respond to the author of this love by seeking daily to live in the light of his Son, Jesus Christ. This is why regular prayer is so important, not only for those who live in religious communities but for everyone. The service of Morning Prayer begins – as it has done for many centuries – with the following verse and response:

> O Lord, open our lips
> And our mouth shall proclaim your praise.

The words come from a psalm[2] written by King David when the prophet Nathan came to him to confront him with his adultery with Bathsheba. She was the wife of an officer in his army whom he had arranged to have killed in order to protect his reputation. It is a very moving psalm, where David pleads for mercy and forgiveness. So this verse is a good one with which to begin the day, even if we aren't in the process of committing adultery ourselves. For to ask God to open our lips is to pray for salvation so that what we say and do in the day that lies ahead may be born of God and not of our fallen passions. Moreover, it reminds us that if we allow God to be the source of our energy – the object of our love in all things – our lives are more likely to reflect his love in the world. And to say this prayer is to proclaim that we seek first of all to bring glory to him rather than to ourselves. And whatever our theology of God might be, to view each day in terms of gift rather than possession is to remind ourselves of the need to make the most of the opportunities that lie ahead of us.

For those of us who find times of prayer in the morning difficult to organize in busy schedules of going to work or taking children to school, for example, this can be a helpful prayer. Saying these two lines as we take our first sip of tea, or wait semi-consciously for the toaster to throw up our bread suitably tanned, or struggle to put on our trainers before jarring the back, hips and knees on tarmac and concrete in the cause of better health, is an offering both of ourselves and our day to God. In a previous chapter we talked about the importance of little, yet vastly significant, prayers such as this. For here we are aware that one of the many fruits of a prayerful life is the ability daily to let go of the dark and demonic influences that force us towards excessive self-promotion or self-justification. Here, instead, we are able to rely prayerfully on the processes of love.

Benedict's second step on the ladder of humility encourages us to seek only the will of God in all things, taking no pleasure in the satisfaction of our own desires (RB 7.31). This follows on naturally from our decision to offer our life daily to him. But it is not as straightforward as it sounds as, deep down in human nature, there is a desire to control God. Rather than allowing him into our lives, we tend to deny his existence – for by doing so we think we can keep control of our lives. Aspects of this resistance to his love can be seen in the opposition Jesus encountered from some of the scribes and Pharisees during his ministry at Capernaum as related in the early chapters of St Mark's Gospel.

First of all the scribes, whose job it was to study the religious law, resented his authority and the way in which his teaching helped others but not themselves. Jesus cast out an unclean spirit from a man, and Mark (1.27) tells us the reaction of the crowd was that, 'They were all amazed, and they kept on asking one another, "What is this? A new teaching – with authority!"' Those who claimed to understand matters of faith envied Jesus' 'power to make a difference'. Sometimes, the Church is slow to acknowledge the power in other religions or non-religious organizations – those who don't live by our traditions – to make a difference to people's lives. Sometimes, too, we can become very suspicious of those who teach or live a different gospel from ours. Or we can become so afraid of letting go that we decide to hold on to unhelpful desires and practices more than ever. We can make such good friends of our negative instincts, we would rather not live without them. Even in the most challenging of times, we refuse to let go. I am reminded of the story of a man who was walking along a cliff path one day when he slipped. He fell over the edge and, hanging on by his finger tips while his body hung hundreds of feet in the air above some jagged rocks below, he prayed earnestly, 'Is there anyone up there? If so, please help me now. I'll do anything for you in the future, if you just save me.' A voice from heaven called down, 'Do not fear. I will look after you. Trust me. Just let go and all will be well.' There was a pause while the man considered this offer after which he cried out again, 'Is there anyone else up there I can talk to?'

Second, these scribes objected to the way Jesus forgave the sins of a paralysed man. As far as they were concerned, the only person who had the power to forgive sins was God. In the increasing absence of belief in a God of judgement today, we no longer fear the eternal consequences of our actions in the way that those who were brought up to fear the wrath of God once were. We tend not to think that either Jesus or God forgives sins, because in the absence of any fear of judgement, there is little accountability. Asking an unseen creator for forgiveness is a crazy concept to many these days. Justice instead belongs to those who uphold and apply the law of the land. But even if we do accept God's power to forgive sins, not least through the teaching of Jesus Christ, we can be offended when others who we feel have tried less hard than ourselves to live a faithful life, seem to claim a degree of forgiveness that we don't feel should be theirs. Apparently, everyone gets to go to heaven these days either because we have realized that the unconditional love of God is for everyone, or we have become afraid to preach about judgement, heaven and hell, or we just don't believe in all that bloodcurdling teaching any more. Yet as soon as we encounter real evil, we cannot conceive of a God who does not punish the appalling wickedness that makes people set fire to a church where women and children have taken refuge, throwing those who escape – including a three-year-old child – back into the flames.[3] To object to the judgement and forgiveness of God might on the one hand be a healthy sign that we are prepared to take responsibility for our actions. But this can never be the whole story, for we can only understand this responsibility in terms of humanity's role in the evolution of life within the purposes of God. To assume this responsibility without acknowledging the existence of a higher authority than ourselves is another sign that we have yet to surrender our desire to control our destiny in favour of developing our trust in the love of God.

Benedict challenges us to understand that a humble life is one where we take responsibility for our actions, their causes and their consequences, wherever this is appropriate. For in our pursuit of humility we come to understand something of how earth relates to heaven and how every life is important to God. We believe the greatest gift that God gives to us is our life. And the greatest response we can make to this gift is to fill it with love. We cannot deny that the witness of the Gospels is constant in its message that everyone has at some stage to give an account of how they have used that gift, for good or ill. So how we live not only affects how we are with others but also how we are with God. We know, too, that to believe in Christ is to find a way of finding forgiveness at least in this life if not in the next as well.

Third, Jesus puts the needs of all people – not just the good, dedicated and respectable – above any need to obey even the most sacred teaching of the religious law. If there is a clash of interests, he puts people first. He is happy to be in the company of irreligious people. This was something the scribes and the Pharisees, who dedicated their lives to practising the religious law as fully as possible, could not agree with. So it comes as no surprise that as early as the beginning of the third chapter of Mark's Gospel his enemies were joining forces to work out how they could destroy Jesus. This reminds us that having a Christian faith can be fine until it conflicts with our own interests. When we have put our faith in a system of belief and in the community of the Church, we do not look kindly on those who challenge our faith. For the most part today we condemn the prophets who force us to reconsider our religious values by faint praise followed by extreme indifference. The history of the Church is full of the trials and condemnation of those who have not kept within the limits of orthodox teaching. In mainstream Christianity, at one level this has helped to preserve the authenticity of our faith for thousands of years. There have been plenty who have claimed their own authority, even setting up their own churches in order to control others. And even in the Church's more liberal approach to belief today, there are still lines that you cannot cross if you are to remain within the fold. But this laudable pursuit of orthodoxy can also exclude those who have been called to make us think afresh about our faith and to make it known anew in our generation. We forget, perhaps, that prophets are supposed to challenge us in order to keep our faith alive. While we rejoice at the way Jesus put people's needs before religious respectability, when someone with an unconventional lifestyle tries to join us, the institutional Church doesn't always cope very well. I once sat anonymously in a congregation, unwashed and unkempt in clothes that smelt as if I was down and out. I received three quite contrasting reactions. There was one person who couldn't do enough for me. Some completely ignored me. And there were others whose reaction was typified by the woman who whenever she came anywhere near me, lifted her scarf to cover her mouth and nose while averting her gaze.

Barbara Glasson, a Methodist minister in Liverpool, describes how she founded a church around a group of unlikely people from the margins of society who got together to bake bread.[4] Instead of trying to knead her people into the shape of conventional Christianity by asking them how their experience fitted within the tradition of the Church, her theological approach was to ask the breadmakers, 'How does this experience change our tradition?' Here holiness is not a 'desired faith outcome' but 'a gentle gift to those who hold and are held'. She does not ask, 'Who belongs to this church?' but rather 'To whom does this church belong?' And the strength of the church is not measured by the numbers it manages to hold on to but by the numbers of those who, renewed by the Spirit, are able to leave it to restart their lives. Moreover, they do not sell the bread they make. They give it away. Barbara writes, 'Faith, like life, begins as a gift not as a doctrine. I move, I breathe, I see, I relate, I love.' It is here, in this earthy place that humility takes root as we allow Divine love to teach us how to love as Christ loves. This kind of earthiness should, therefore, be present somewhere in every Christian community and as an aspect of the faith of every devoted follower of Christ. For when we manage to sit light to the religious paraphernalia we rely on so much, we are able to ascend to heaven free of any vested interests that might tie us down.

So part of the process of letting go is to strike a balance between the predictability we need in order to lead an organized life and the unpredictability of God. Jesus reminds us that the Spirit of God blows like a wind through creation in an undetermined manner,[5] so we need to be constantly open to new possibilities of love. And as we are constantly challenged to let go of unhelpful beliefs and practices, we need especially to release ourselves from our desire to control God.

We have to let go of any concept of Christianity that presents God in terms of a service provider who is on the end of a phone and, without so much as a call-out charge, will instantly come to our rescue whenever we are in pain. And we need to hold on to the divinity that emerges when we doggedly pursue the Spirit of Christ among the mess that most of us make of life. For the healing of our spirits has little to do with our selfish pursuit of pleasure without pain. It has a great deal to do with the long-term growth that takes place when we embrace the pain of the world with love. Here love does not necessarily take the pain away but it is the best way we can cope with it and the only way we can redeem it. For while we cannot have all the experiences and sensations we think we want or need in this life to make us feel good, we are likely to be given other opportunities to quicken our souls. And as we have seen, the priority of the Christian journey is the ascent of our lives into God through humility and prayerful self-offering. To ignore the pursuit of these aims so helpfully expressed by Benedict is to deprive the world of the hope of redemption.

To be a Christian is not to have arrived in a perfect place of personal development nor is it to be better than anyone else. To be a Christian is to be open and committed to the purposes of Divine love and its redeeming work in creation. Yet as we find increasingly the freedom of spirit and ascent into Christ that comes from serving others, we will inevitably continue to make mistakes. We will lose our tempers, make uncharitable remarks, behave badly in the company of others, we will swear, forget to say our prayers and wonder at times whether this faith makes any real difference at all. But instead of condemning ourselves or thinking that we have somehow failed God, we will regard these highs and lows as the essence of the spiritual life. Doubt and denial are part of faith and we live with them as we live with hope and love. It came as a surprise to some but not to those who live with this kind of integrity of faith when it was revealed that Mother Teresa, a great saint of our times, for decades had lived with great doubts about her faith in Jesus Christ while at the same time serving him sacrificially day by day in her service of the poorest of the poor. Sainthood, she reminds us, is not about certainty but about faithful love in all circumstances and not least when your heart is breaking. And hope is not about always looking back to take our reference from the past but about becoming involved in the dynamics of the unfolding love of God where little is assured. As Sara Maitland reminds us,

If I have correctly understood the contingent nature of so much of our knowledge, the ground of our *hope* can no longer rest on some promise given in the past, of future security as a reward for good behaviour in the present. Hope lies rather in accepting that God's engagement in the creation gives us not just the right, but the obligation to create and sustain the future.[6]

There will always be those who want to put limits on the love of God by linking it with certainty. This is often a sign of their personal and spiritual immaturity and their childish desire for answers, security and protection. They convince a few who are similar to themselves but they make many grown-ups believe it's not worth bothering. So desperate are they to conjure up a God who can deal with their doubts and insecurity, they ask us whether we have 'a personal relationship with Jesus'. This can leave those of us who don't have his private email address feeling in danger of being deleted from the heavenly hard drive of salvation. I am not saying that we cannot have a personal relationship with Jesus Christ or that this is undesirable. Far from it. For relating personally to the Spirit of Christ in creation has always been part of what it means to be a Christian. But we need to let go of any idea that Jesus is our personal adviser in all circumstances, otherwise we might, for example, make some disastrous decisions in our relationships or in planning our future. If we think that he is at our beck and call to this degree, why shouldn't he advise us personally about ethical financial investments as much as personal morality? There may well be specific times when God 'speaks to us', in our hearts and minds. But if we think he is constantly at our beck and call, we may discover that in casting Jesus in the role of personal adviser, we have underestimated the power of the brain to conjure up voices from within itself. We discover that we have been talking to ourselves. For those of us who cannot fit our faith into little boxes of tight-lipped dogma, experience of the authentic love of God often – usually – comes as much through our experience of failure or even godlessness as it does through any sense of the risen Christ standing by our side. It is here that we realize Christian faith and love in this world can never be the preserve of the perfect. It can only be for those who acknowledge their inherent weaknesses. For certainty suffocates the Spirit of love. In time and by great devotion and humility, we may achieve that communion with the love of God that will render us irrelevant to mainstream society as we ascend ever further to the heavenly places. Most of us, on the other hand, muddle our way through, faithful and faithless, loving and loveless, from day to day. But this is a glorious undertaking because, made in the image of God, we are of intrinsic worth and loved by God as his children. For 'When God looks at a person, He does not see either virtue, which may not exist, or success, which may not have been achieved, but He sees the unshakeable shining beauty of His own image.'[7] So through these mists we can make out not only the love of God but also a destiny that means we can begin to see beyond the horizons of this life.

As Jacob prayed at night in a desert place, we notice how in the early ministry of Jesus at Capernaum – to which we referred above – he went out early in the morning when it is very dark, to pray in a deserted place.[8] We might imagine that here, too, in the quiet Galilean countryside there was a ladder that reached up to heaven from where Jesus stood in prayer. It reminds us also of our need to ascend into the presence of God through the ladder of our humility and faltering prayers.

\* \* \*

## From the Rule of St Benedict

Truly, we are forbidden to do our own will, for the Scripture tells us: 'Turn away from your desires' (Sir 18.30). And in the Prayer too we ask God that his 'will be done' in us (Matt 6.10). (Part of the first step of humility, RB 7.19–20).

# *For reflection*

He [Poemen] also said, 'Humility is the ground on which the Lord ordered the sacrifice to be offered.'[9]

Are there aspects of my faith that I need to let go of so that I can understand more fully the love of God?

## Something to do

Have a look at your work–life balance to see if there are times when you fail to give serious consideration to the needs of others. If need be, resolve to spend more time with your spouse, partner, family or friends. Go out of your way to spend some time with those you should be with.

## A Bible passage to consider

And as he sat at dinner in the house, many tax collectors and sinners came and were sitting with him and his disciples. When the Pharisees saw this, they said to his disciples, 'Why does your teacher eat with tax collectors and sinners?' But when he heard this, he said, 'Those who are well have no need of a physician, but those who are sick. Go and learn what this means, "I desire mercy, not sacrifice." For I have come to call not the righteous but sinners.' (Matthew 9.10–13)

## Prayer

Thy will be done
not mine
but thine.

# 11

## *The desire to live for ever*

————◆————

The French Jesuit priest, palaeontologist and theologian, Pierre
Teilhard de Chardin, in his autobiography, which he wrote late in
his life, recalls the moment in his childhood when he realized his
mortality. He was five years old and sitting by the fire while his
mother was cutting his hair. He saw a piece of hair fall from the
scissors into the fire and quickly disintegrate in the intense heat:

> The child was seized with horror and disgust. What was
> disappearing, he suddenly realised, was part of himself –
> curling like an autumn leaf, turning into nothing. 'An awful
> feeling came on me at that moment,' he later wrote. 'For the
> first time in my life I *knew* I was perishable.'

He was deeply upset by this and lying in his mother's arms as she
comforted him, he knew 'he had to find some personal security
in a world that fell to dust and ash so easily.'[1]

Teilhard went on to become a distinguished author and lecturer
who was constantly under pressure to moderate his views so that
they fell in line with the traditions and teaching of the Roman
Catholic Church. He believed that science and religion were not
incompatible and that one informed the other. He also felt that in
terms of the evolution of humanity, human beings had reached a
point where they needed to add to their belief of Jesus Christ –
as God made man and Word made flesh – to understand him more
fully as the universal Christ. Describing our relationship with Christ,
he says that where spirit and matter fuse into one, 'whether we
like it or not by power and by right you are incarnate in the world,

and we are all of us dependent upon you'.[2] The cross is not so much to do with atonement or even redemption but 'is the symbol of progress and victory won through mistakes, disappointments and hard work'.[3] Here 'the two components of the future are synthesized: the transcendent and the ultra-human . . . the Above and the Ahead'.[4] He preferred to think of the fulfilment of history not so much in terms of a picture of a final banquet and the physical return of Christ to the world but more in terms of it being the Omega point to which all paths lead. Evolution is an ascent towards its fulfilment in a harmonized 'super-consciousness'[5] covering the earth, a bit like the Internet today.

This rather impersonal representation of the ascent of humanity towards its final destiny seems a long way from traditional biblical images of the end time such as we read about in the Gospels that are full of imagery from the Hebrew culture of the first century. It is not surprising that his ideas were too unorthodox for many in his day. (He died in 1955.) Many still feel he was an errant priest who wandered away from orthodox faith but others see him as one who combined a sense of Gaia and God. He reinterpreted the Christian faith for the modern mind. It is without doubt that through his freedom of thought and radical approach in reconciling the gospel to the modern mind, Teilhard gave others permission to think about their faith in a new way. He spoke to many in his day who felt that a purely traditional reaction to the life of Christ – divorced from the developing spiritual and intellectual evolution of humanity – was likely to consign him and the Church to history. And there are many devout Christians today who also believe they are called to push the boundaries of faith towards a fresh understanding of Christ.

Reflection on the transient nature of life is not, of course, confined to priests, scientists or theologians. Anyone at a very young age, seeing his hair burn in a fire, may well be provoked by the experience to try and discover later on the meaning behind his or her existence. Teilhard de Chardin's experience of the fragility of life probably became most acute when he was an army chaplain in the trenches of the First World War, and there will be innumerable children all over the world who, as a result of civil or military violence and the loss of loved ones and friends, will have been prompted to think about the significance of their life and the lives of the loved ones they have lost.

The desire to understand these things can also arise from our observations of the transience of certain aspects of human nature. On the whole, we struggle to be good yet sometimes – in a moment of heated discussion – can do and say things that we do not mean and would not normally say. We are aware that we can conduct ourselves in a perfectly civilized manner most of the time. But given sufficient pressure, we can behave in a way that we describe as being 'completely out of character'. How can ethnic groups who have lived peacefully side by side for years suddenly turn against each other? When my safety is threatened, why does inherited instinctual behaviour override my sense of justice? Feelings of altruism can soon be lost in the hellish stampede of those trying to escape a life-threatening situation. While one would never normally walk over someone else lying on the ground, this can be almost inevitable in the headlong rush to escape a burning plane or a sports ground where a crowd is out of control. Here my behaviour is controlled and defined by the need to survive at all costs, and extreme circumstances trigger an instinct to put myself before others. Confronted by the aggression of others, I may also become consumed by the hatred of the aims of others, coupled with my desire to get even. And, ironically, a fundamentalist distortion of my faith for my own ends can give me the permission I need to consider others less worthy of life than I. And there is nothing more deadly than the closed mind of the fundamentalist who has unwittingly combined instinctual behaviour with religious fanaticism.

Yet there are those who in life-threatening circumstances chose another way. They are able to lay aside the need to survive and are prepared to sacrifice their lives – not for any reward in heaven, but simply so that others might live. They somehow manage to convert their innate and sometimes destructive desires by a love that transcends natural instincts. When compared with the way people naturally behave, their love of humanity – surfacing sometimes in very unlikely situations – appears to belong, as it were, to another world. An army chaplain on a torpedoed troop carrier that was sinking in mid-Atlantic in the Second World War refused to save himself. There were not enough lifeboats for everyone. Many of the men he served were about to drown. He declined the offer to enter one of the lifeboats and decided instead to remain with those left behind and go down with the ship.

The desire to survive when surrendered to the Spirit of Christ – the Spirit of creative love of the universe that renders our ambitions either dormant or divinely inspired – is where Divine creative love emerges in the world. Here the desire to live with a false sense of our immortality or for selfish gain yields to the desire to forsake certainty and even safety in the pursuit of the way of Divine love into what we might describe as 'the Above and Ahead'. This is an exciting prospect, as it appears that in the denial of what we might call carnal desires lies the way of redemption. But is this the preserve of intellectual giants alone – such as Teilhard de Chardin – who can rationalize their way through humanity's innate behavioural systems? I suspect not. For it is far more likely and more in line with the Christian gospel that this way is open to anyone who is prepared to live by sacrificial love. But how do we do this?

There is, of course, no easy answer. But we may be sure that to live by the natural desire to survive and without love of others leads to a very self-centred existence and one in which we are content to tread on others to get what we want. We can see how this operates in the marketplace of life, where we are very selective in the way we relate to others. We may feel love for those at home but our relations with business competitors can quickly be governed by the laws relating to the survival of the fittest. So to live by sacrificial love involves some very difficult decisions that may cost us dearly both in terms of our relationships with others and also our business interests and income. In order to pursue the love that leads us to eternal life we are likely to find, therefore, that we need to move our lives in a new direction. That is, we have to decide not only to put our innate drive towards the survival of the fittest into neutral but also to subject all our other desires and negative passions to love. For the Christian, this means making a decision to follow Christ daily. This is not simply deciding to make further enquiries but to walk in the footsteps of Christ and to learn how to love as Christ loves. In this sense we cannot be both of the world – content to live according to our fallen desires while claiming to belong to Christ – and pursue the way of sacrificial love. Our lives reflect the choices we have made. To paraphrase Jesus, 'You are either for or against me, you cannot put all your hope in this world and also in me. You cannot have both. If you know what is good for you, opt for life rather than death.'[6]

When we do decide to follow Christ, this does not mean, however, that our earthbound desires will suddenly, if ever, be completely replaced by holy desires. But it does mean that in 'the pursuit of love at the expense of evil' we will discover a life that not even death can destroy.

In the Gospels this is called the way of eternal life. It forms a particular theme in the Fourth Gospel, where we read, 'For God so loved the world that he gave his only Son, so that everyone who believes in him may not perish but may have eternal life.'[7] The concept of eternal life in the teaching of Jesus Christ, and especially in the mystery of his cross and resurrection, provides a new understanding of life that is available for those who are prepared to take a step in the right direction. But what does this mean? For countless Christians have lived and died and remain in this world only in the memories of those who are alive today who themselves will eventually die. But eternal life as the Gospels describe it is not a description of living for ever in terms of a continued temporal existence. It has more to do with being caught up in the life of God in this world and the next, in the Above and the Ahead.

If we are going to ask people to reorientate their lives from self-preservation to self-sacrifice, most will expect us to provide some proof for them that what is being offered here is true. When you speak to young people today, many of whom are caught up in a highly hedonistic culture, about the new possibilities for life that Christian faith brings, you can understand their incredulity at the lack of tangible proof. They live in a materialistic society where there is a great emphasis on the acquisition and maintenance of the wealth they believe they need to be happy and secure. This is nothing new, of course, for they share their desire for proof with countless souls of all ages in previous generations who have preferred to believe in what they can see and prove to be true.

St Augustine (354–430), Bishop of Hippo in North Africa and one of the principal theologians of the early Church, became a convert to Christianity at the age of 32, having been profoundly moved by the life of St Anthony of the Desert.[8] It is as if St Anthony gave Augustine permission to come to terms with the demons of his life and so become incorporated into the love of Christ. His new-found understanding of God led Augustine to write:

> O God, you who are so high above us and yet so close, hidden and yet always present, you have not parts, some greater and some smaller. You are everywhere, and everywhere you are entire. Nowhere are you limited by space. You have not the shape of a body like ours. Yet you made man in your own likeness, and man is plainly in space from head to foot.[9]

Until that point, Augustine had lived a fairly self-centred lifestyle and fathered a child out of wedlock. Yet he became convinced both of the omnipresence of God and also of the uniqueness of the cross and resurrection in terms of what it was reasonable and necessary to believe. For Augustine, one of the principal ways in which you found the proof you were looking for was in the faith of others. Their faith and love gave you permission to believe. In this sense, both faith and eternal life are gifts which others offer us. St Augustine says:

The world has believed a tiny number of men of low birth, low position, with no academic qualifications; and it has believed them just because in the persons of such insignificant witnesses the power of God exercised a much more wonderful persuasion. What I mean is that those who persuaded men of this truth did so by utterances which on their lips were turned into miracles, rather than mere words.[10]

We cannot underestimate the significance, therefore, of the Christ-centred life, in terms of the effect it can have on others.

Through the writing of St Augustine, many came to believe, and both he and St Anthony – among others – gave Benedict permission to believe. He trusted in their words and witness when he found they made sense of himself and his mortal existence. Their faith, and the faith of many others, forced him to conclude that if you were prepared to trust what they had to say, you had to change the direction of your life.

This, of course, is what Bendict's Rule is for. It offers those who have been given permission to believe, a way to set about living a new life. For faith and practice have to go together. 'A brother said to Anthony, "Pray for me." He answered, "Neither I nor God will have mercy on you unless you do something about it yourself and ask God's help." '[11]

The outcome of faith in a person's life, however, is far more glorious than any personal gain. Faith leads to a new way of life for the Christian – be he or she a religious or layperson – so that we no longer live for ourselves but for God. St Peter reminds us, 'Since therefore Christ suffered in the flesh, arm yourselves with the same intention . . . so as to live for the rest of your earthly life no longer by human desires but by the will of God.'[12] But this does not mean, as some would have us believe, that our freedom becomes bound up in slavish obedience to rules and regulations which remind us more of our innate human fallibility than of our faithfulness. Nor does having this faith mean that we belong to an exclusive club – the Church – where we regard those outside as inferior. Authentic faith means, instead, that we become so engaged in the life of God that he releases godliness not only into our lives but also and especially into the life of the world. He who is unlimited by space creates space for new life that bears his eternal image. Recognizing this divine life developing within himself, St Paul felt moved to write, 'it is no longer I who live but Christ who lives in me'.[13] Again, Paul is not saying that he didn't have his own life any more but that the universal Spirit of Christ – the Spirit of resurrection and redemption – was becoming such a part of his life that he could no longer be fully himself without being fully inspired and enlivened by the Holy Spirit.

For anyone contemplating the meaning of the Christian life, this is exciting news. And when we have been faithful over many years, it can be helpful to review where our spiritual journey has taken us and decide whether we need to rediscover something of the energy and excitement of our first commitment. At other times, it is helpful to explain to those who are on the fringes of this faith that taking this step is not a matter of being concerned with ourselves. It does not stop with our own personal salvation, important though this is. And it is unhelpful to think about our faith only in terms of our safety, our ability to get through this life and into the next with God. For when we grow in faith and become incorporated into the life of Christ, we are caught up in the divine energies of redemption. The principal way we do this is through sacrificial love where the desires of the world are crucified through our love for God. And the place where we begin is in self-offering rather than political engagement, social action, charitable works, or theological learning.

Living in a culture where there is a high emphasis on activism, we can overlook the power that the redeemed lover releases into the community and into the world. We forget that prayerful attentiveness at the foot of the cross is where any ideas of mission, evangelism and redemption receive their energy and vision. And this prayer of self-offering cannot be a one-off event, for this kind of focus is easily wrested from our grasp by the demands of everyday life. So we have to travel to the foot of the cross almost daily in the knowledge that here – in the unlikely place of deadly desires – we can find and name a love that lasts for ever. Here is the Divine love that will transform the tomb of selfish desire into the womb of eternal life. St Benedict makes the focus of the Christian life clear at the end of the Prologue to his Rule when he says, 'Never swerving from his instructions, then, but faithfully observing his teaching in the monastery until death, we shall through patience share in the sufferings of Christ that we may deserve also to share in his kingdom' (RB Prologue 50).

The point at which we live this life of Christ where eternal possibilities confront the pressures of daily living, combines both wonder at the greatness of creation and a desire to further the purposes of God. Here, by grace, we are given the faith to journey towards a destiny that lies beyond the horizon of human comprehension. Jesus himself, as the archetypal person of faith, did not know the times and seasons of the love of God[14] and this was true even on the cross.[15] But our prayerful engagement in life comes not from the certainty of the outcome of love but in our assured commitment to its sometimes hazardous pursuit, because we have become faithfully aware that herein lies the secret of redemption. So our faith is forged somewhere between reasonable belief and a lack of final understanding. And while the statement of that faith may develop from one generation to the next, it remains the truth so long as it leads men and women to God through the love of Jesus Christ. The revelation of the love of God in Jesus Christ is sufficient for us to know eternal life while it is extremely unlikely that we will ever be able to comprehend this mystery in all its fullness.

Jesus describes the nature and consequence of Christian discipleship in the following terms, 'For everyone will be salted with fire. Salt is good; but if salt has lost its saltiness, how can you season it? Have salt in yourselves and be at peace with one another.'[16] It may seem remarkable that Jesus spoke here in terms of salt but this may have been because in his day salt was used as a preservative for food and it was also a symbol of purity. While salt appears to be insignificant, even the smallest amount is noticeable when used.

In further consideration of this salt, and given what we have said above concerning the unfathomable nature of the love of God and the engagement in redemption to which we have been called, I am reminded of some words quoted by Michael Mayne, who himself maintained his faith in the face of great suffering and terminal illness. Mayne refers to Carl Sagan, Professor of Astronomy and Space Science at Cornell University, who asks whether we can know 'ultimately and in every detail' even a grain of salt:

> [For] one microgram of table salt, a single just visible speck, contains 1016 atoms of sodium and chlorine. That's a 1 followed by 16 zeros, 10 million billion atoms. To say nothing of the forces holding these atoms together. And each atom, rank upon rank of them, are 'in an ordered array, a regularly alternating structure'.

Sagan goes on to conclude that the amount of information that can be known by the human brain, given its make-up and function, is no more than one per cent of the number of atoms in a grain of salt. So our hope of ever fully understanding the universe is slim.[17]

This, in turn, reminds me of a story Mother Teresa once told that involved a bag of salt. She had taken into one of her homes a young boy whom she had found emaciated and dying in the gutter. In time, she and her Sisters nursed him back to health. Eventually he was strong and well enough to return to the streets. As he came to leave, Mother Teresa gave him a bag of salt, as was her custom. Salt was expensive and therefore this gift represented some short-term financial security for the boy as he began his life again in his community. As the boy was leaving, he passed another youngster – being carried into the home on a stretcher – who was in pretty much the same state as he had been when Mother Teresa first rescued him. As he passed the stretcher, he placed his bag of salt next to the sick boy. Mother Teresa asked him why he had done this. The healthy boy replied that while he was healthy again, the sick boy was in greater need of help than he, so he gave him the only thing he had.

It is strange that something as relatively insignificant as salt could become a symbol both of the unfathomable nature of the universe and also in a Calcutta slum of the nature of the sacrificial love that alone redeems the world. When Divine love is given expression in humanity, our life is radically changed. Here heavenly possibilities are discovered and released through the most simple words and actions. As the boy placed his bag of salt on the stretcher, it is as if his spirit – his essential self – had also returned from death to life. He could so easily have held on to the salt and made the excuse that Mother Teresa and her Sisters were bound also to help the boy on the stretcher. But there is something in the giving of what we have – sometimes all that we have – that in itself raises us up to new life. The boy's final healing – his resurrection – came about through this self-offering. He gave more than a commodity that could be bought and sold. He gave away his security and maybe even his life and health. In short, he gave himself. And, dare we claim, it is this kind of loving to which we have also been called. For we who are so well off have, I suspect, much to learn from this young boy who lived in great poverty. For even in a grain of salt, the unfathomable heights and depths of heaven and earth, the known and knowable, the life that is in space and beyond space, meet and become one. This is, I presume, what St Paul is getting at when he writes:

> I pray that you may have the power to comprehend, with all the saints, what is the breadth and length and height and depth, and to know the love of Christ that surpasses knowledge, so that you may be filled with all the fullness of God.[18]

While we may not have the final proof of God and eternity we would like, our wonder at the mystery of life and our faithful pursuit of creative love can give us the permission we need to believe in the one who calls himself 'The way, and the truth, and the life'.[19] We are not committing spiritual or mental suicide if we believe in Christ. Quite the opposite. For by this faith we learn how to live for ever.

Teilhard de Chardin was an outstanding scientist in his own field and, while he expressed his understanding of eternal life in terms of a cosmic mind or consciousness, he was able nevertheless to remain most intimate with God in prayer. 'I shall gather into a single prayer', he writes, 'both my delight in what I have and my thirst for what I lack.' He goes on to pray:

> Lord, lock me up in the deepest depths of your heart; and then, holding me there, burn me, purify me, set me on fire, sublimate me, till I become utterly what you would have me be, through the utter annihilation of my ego.[20]

Having given ourselves permission to believe, and through our engagement in the life of God stepped into the life of eternity, we find that earth and heaven meet when Christ becomes incarnate in self-offering love. We discover also the centre of our prayers in which we hold together the joys and tensions of that love – what we have and what we long to possess – which consist of a heart-felt embrace. Here as Divine Spirit and human spirit become increasingly indistinguishable, we give God permission to live through us. It is to this Divine prayerful embrace that we shall return in our final chapter.

\* \* \*

## From the Rule of St Benedict

What is not possible to us by nature, let us ask the Lord to supply by the help of his grace. If we wish to reach eternal life, even as we avoid the torments of hell, then – while there is still time, while we are in this body and have time to accomplish all these things by the light of life – we must run and do now what will profit us forever. (RB Prologue 41–44)

## *For reflection*

If with Christ you died to the elemental spirits of the universe, why do you live as if you still belonged to the world? (Colossians 2.20)

Sometimes we live in a very self-centred way. We mould the gospel around our desire for power or our insecurities. We follow our religious ways but leave our self-indulgence unchecked. How true is this of you at this time in your life?

Spend some time on your own or in discussion with others and reflect on the ways in which we should offer a different way of life to others.

### Something to do

The next time you put salt on your food or just take some salt and hold it in your hand, study the grains for a while and reflect on your calling to make a difference to the world. You might also like to consider the amazing intricacies of creation and the wonder of God's love for you.

### A Bible passage to consider

My sheep hear my voice. I know them, and they follow me. I give them eternal life, and they will never perish. No one will snatch them out of my hand. What my Father has given me is greater than all else, and no one can snatch it out of my Father's hand. The Father and I are one. (John 10.27–30: Jesus' last saying before the raising of Lazarus)

## Prayer

Father of the universe,
thank you for the works of your hands
and the wonders of your love.
May I become as salt
in my service of others
that through the offering of myself
they may come to know
the life that lasts for ever.

# 12

## *The love that keeps you in touch*

It is not difficult at times to focus on the joys of being alive just as it is not difficult at times to become more negative about suffering and the fragility of life. Nor is it difficult to find oneself occasionally wandering aimlessly through life, wondering what on earth – or heaven – it is about. We also find it easy and quite natural to shape our beliefs – about ourselves, God, the world and the universe – according to our mood at any one moment. On a bright sunny weekend break, we may feel that God is in heaven and all is well in the world. Lying in a hospital bed, we might be given to feelings of fear and godlessness. On the grey days of life, when the rain is battering incessantly at the window, and nature appears to be dormant and uninterested in the approach of another spring, God is seldom seen as anything other than shades of grey.

Through these different times and experiences we can discover different aspects of our faith and understanding of the nature of God whose creation reflects the many aspects of his joy, pain and love. Among these broad areas of human experience, there are times that we rarely look for or expect, when God, as it were, creeps up on us unexpected. We can find ourselves reflecting later on the words of what at the time appeared to be an innocuous conversation discovering within them a significance that goes beyond our immediate world of sensory experience. Or we may suddenly be given to understand or appreciate somebody we know very well in a new light. For a moment we may see something in or around them that speaks to us of angels and of heaven, or of a divine reality hitherto unrecognized, even when we would not normally assent to the existence of such things. These experiences may well teach us something about the nature of God, but more often they are given simply to guide us at significant times in our lives. For the most part in themselves, they convince us – beyond words or reason – that there is more to life than meets the eye.

I wonder what the result would be if someone were to ask us to go away on our own and, without any other influences, including our Christian faith, put together a coherent picture of God from these experiences? The chances are that we would come up with an understanding of God similar to that of a primitive religion. Few of us, without the influence of the Church or other Christians and their revelation of Christ, would speak about God in terms of the Father, Son and Holy Spirit which in the Church formed the foundation of Trinitarian belief from very early on. So while our experiences of God in daily life are both valid and significant, they receive their fullness of meaning through our faith in Jesus Christ. This is what Paul is saying when he addresses the members of the Greek learned classes as they debate weighty matters of philosophy and belief in the marketplace in Athens. He tells them that the God they worship does not consist of stone or metal effigy but is revealed instead in the life, death and resurrection of Jesus Christ. Moreover, this is the God in whom 'we live and move and have our being'.[1]

It is an astonishing claim – considered arrogant by many – that Paul, or anyone for that matter, should tell others about the God who is really behind their faith. It is a claim based on the belief that something unique happened to humanity through the incarnation of Christ, when humanity apprehended the fullness of the love of God in human form. For Paul, intellectual though he was, did not claim to speak about access to the truth by superior knowledge and learning, but by humility and love. Rather than mocking the inadequacies of someone else's faith, he endeavoured to bring out the fullness of meaning that lies behind an authentic experience of God. And this is the role of the Church today. For we give to others a framework of love – defined by certain core beliefs, prayer and a way of life – that we hope gives shape and meaning to the godly experience of others. By this we hope that they will find fullness of meaning in their faith and fullness of life in their understanding of themselves. The effect this love has on us is to liberate our spirits from constantly being dragged up and down through the highs and lows of life, the joys and sorrows that are central to our human experience. I am not suggesting that we will no longer suffer from doubt and times of godlessness but that in times of light and darkness we will continue to believe and deep down know that God is with us. Here our faith finds its fullness of meaning as we awake to the constancy of the love of God. When our love for him becomes intertwined with his love for us, through prayer and contemplation, they form a continuous thread from day to day, week to week and month to month. To live in the love of Christ, therefore, is to be in touch with God and with the world and others in an embrace of life and death that is no longer fickle and heavily susceptible to the fortunes of life, but is faithful.

In the preceding chapter we looked at our desire for God. In this chapter we can see how our desire for God and our longing for love come together as we seek and find our communion with him. Part of our experience of conversion that precedes our enjoyment of this communion, as we have seen, happens when we give ourselves permission to believe. Instead of holding out on God, we decide to hold on to him. We are helped in this by others who we know or who have gone before us in faith. Their example has helped to break down the walls of self-centred interest, normally regarded as crucial for our survival in the jungle of competing interests in a competitive society. Before, we lived by taking and holding on to whatever society told us we needed. Now we discover a love that comes from giving and letting go. But in case our understanding of the love of Christ is reduced to the level of an alternative medicine designed to cure even the worst spiritual hangovers, we need to remind ourselves of the environment in which this love emerges.

If we are to grow in the love of Christ, we have to take the presence of evil very seriously. For love emerges only through the thicket of natural instincts that orientate human behaviour towards the survival of the fittest and the chaos these instincts cause in the lives of others and ourselves. At its worst, evil can pollute and permanently disfigure us, especially when love goes wrong. Human nature contains a sometimes strange and often awkward juxtaposition between the desire for survival and the longing for love. As God desires the love of his creation to find its fulfilment in him, so the divine nature in us seeks the fruition of that love in our lives. Most of us want to be loved. In being loved by others, we find we are able to love ourselves. When love is shared we feel in touch with heaven and a sense of eternity seems to break into our relationships, for love in its very nature is eternal. It is probably the most important part of our lives. If you are in a relationship of love, relative wealth and poverty become irrelevant so long as you have each other. Love sets our hearts on fire and provides meaning, purpose and new identity. It is the most precious commodity among human beings and in creation because love – and love alone – redeems a fallen world. Perhaps this is why, when love goes wrong, the consequences can be of demonic proportions. For by love we ascend into the presence of God and stay there, but without love we are nothing and descend to live only in the depths of our fallen desires.

Sometimes when love is misunderstood or distorted, the only way we can react is by becoming twisted in our relationships with others because of our anger, pain and bitterness. We are unable to find a better way to react because we have not previously given ourselves permission to grow much beyond instinctual behaviour. While often unspoken and largely unacknowledged, our reactions to the abuse of love can have a very considerable and far-reaching effect on our lives. And whenever we are forced to stop and think about how evil has affected us, we are astonished at the hold it has taken. While we have referred to this in an earlier chapter, as we seek to keep in touch with the love that leads to fullness of life, we need to take definite steps – daily if need be – to walk away from evil when it seeks to demonize us. This is why at the very beginning of his Rule, St Benedict describes the life of the monk in terms of warfare:

> This message of mine is for you, then, if you are ready to give up your own will, once and for all, and armed with the strong and noble weapons of obedience to do battle for the true King, Christ the Lord. (RB Prologue 3)

St Antony, whose life and teaching inspired St Benedict, in his final words to the two men who were looking after him before he died said:

> Be watchful and do not destroy your lengthy discipline, but as if you were making a beginning now, strive to preserve your enthusiasm. You know the treacherous demons – you know how savage they are, even though weakened in strength. Therefore, do not fear them, but rather draw inspiration from Christ always, and trust in him. And live as though dying daily, paying heed to yourselves and remembering what you heard from my preaching.'[2]

Inevitably, therefore, as we pursue the love that redeems the world at the expense of evil, we are led inexorably to the foot of the cross.

We sometimes speak of love almost as if it belongs exclusively to God, and pain almost as if it belongs exclusively to humanity. But the concept that God is good and loving and man is responsible for all the evil in the world overlooks the responsibility God bears for creation in the first place. So pain must lie at the heart of a loving creator God because of the way in which many aspects of his creation have turned out. For many, the cross is seen as the most powerful expression of the love of God who 'gave his only

Son for the sins of the world'. Here God sacrifices what is most precious to himself in the hope that humanity might find it in its heart to ask his forgiveness and avoid ultimate destruction. The emphasis here is on the love of God and the pain of the world where – while there is great suffering for Christ – the redeeming love of God leaves the Father in heaven fairly untouched. But the cross can also be seen as the most powerful expression of the pain of God in creation. It reveals in the stark human form of the dying Christ, the labour pains of God. Here, we can observe the creative Spirit of God continuously working throughout the universe towards greater growth and development, where divine possibilities for life are constantly threatened by demonic influences for death. So there is a cross at the heart of creation, at the very centre of the life of God, and in the heart of our desire to love.

At the foot of the cross the love of humanity is represented by Mary, the Mother of Jesus, John the Beloved Disciple and the other women who watch and wait. Here is the divine life of humanity as it seeks to respond to the pain of God. In this longing to keep in touch with Christ, we are responding to the indwelling Spirit who seeks our union with God in this world and the next. His love in us causes us to want to serve his purposes on earth and in heaven. At the foot of the cross we are more in touch with both the love and the pain of God than we sometimes suppose. So we try and live according to the Spirit rather than according to the desires of the flesh. Here as we comfort one another in the face of an unfathomable darkness, we tend the wounds of Christ. Here we find ourselves not so much fearful of condemnation and begging for forgiveness but crying out to comfort the crucified lover of creation. Esther de Waal reminds us that 'the praise of God is the criterion of the Benedictine life'[3] and we can now appreciate that this praise does not only consist of our duty to 'give God due respect'. For the praise of God also consists of our self-offering, as we respond to both the love and the pain of God in creation. Praise is not, therefore, something that we do simply when we feel good or things are going right or even when we feel the need to acknowledge the greatness of God. Sometimes there is no better place to praise God than in the darkness at the foot of the cross where love's embrace becomes even more passionate because it involves suffering.

The title of the final chapter of the Rule reminds us that to adopt this way of life is only the beginning of perfection, the start of our journey into God. The Rule not only acts as a guide in the dedication of our lives to God, it is also an exhortation to continue to follow a way of life. This is the way along which we will fulfil our destiny by living increasingly prayerfully with Christ on a daily basis. One of the most important ways by which we keep in touch with God, is prayerful reading of Holy Scripture and other spiritual writings. This has always formed a basis for the Benedictine life, as it does today.[4]

This reading consists principally of the Old and New Testaments and the teachings of the holy Fathers.[5] In Benedictine spirituality it is referred to as *lectio divina*[6], which consisted in the early days of one monk reading Holy Scripture for the others to listen to. In time, as books became more available, it came to refer both to times of public reading and also to times of personal spiritual reading. Today, for those who wish to follow a Benedictine way of life outside a monastery, times of personal *lectio divina* – where spiritual reading and prayer combine – can form the foundation of the spiritual life.[7] The particular structure and practice of *lectio divina* of the Bible which the Benedictines use is especially helpful in the way it leaves less room than some methods for well-intentioned but dangerous misuse of Bible passages.[8] While it is not the aim here to go into the art of *lectio divina* in any great detail, it is worth noting that its structure is fourfold. First, we take a passage of Scripture, read it and absorb it into our mind and then spend some time reflecting on its significance and meaning. This leads us into a response of prayer, after which we move into wordless contemplation and adoration as we move closer to God. This in turn will challenge us to incorporate something of our divine reading into our daily lives and further help us to participate in Holy Communion where through bread and wine we become one with God.

Sitting down in peace and quiet to read and pray the Holy Scriptures can become an invaluable source of comfort, insight and joy. There are occasions when words, as it were, leap off the page to give us fresh insight into the grace of God and the meaning of our lives. At other times, we may feel we can visualize the Gospel stories as if we were there and 'see' Christ next to us. More often, we may struggle with some passage that makes little sense. When in frustration we are ready to give up we find our spirits suddenly refreshed as it were from beyond ourselves, highlighting the meaning of a passage in a new way. But all spiritual reading should come with a strong health warning. We can easily misread the Bible through a lack of knowledge or understanding of the kind of Scripture we are dealing with. Or we can impose our own ideas on to the text in a godless manner which through spiritual superficiality leads us to imprison ourselves and others in lies rather than setting ourselves free in the truth. This is why the Benedictine method of *lectio divina* is so helpful, for it demands that we take this reading very seriously. We cannot dabble with it, dipping in and out while selecting favourite passages or verses. It makes us sit very still and wrestle with ourselves as much as with the text. And because it is so exacting, it forces us to relate what we read to what we say in prayer and to our daily lives. While it is by no means foolproof, if we are prepared to learn how to use this method of holy reading, we are not as likely to lose our way as when we use a less demanding method.

Anyone who has spent a sustained period of time in a religious house knows how centring and also how demanding this kind of Bible reading can be. Everything – the whole day – revolves around prayer and spiritual reading. Prayer ceases to be a private activity whereby I get God to talk to me about my life. Instead it becomes a ceaseless round of praise and worship for God's sake not ours. This can leave us feeling exposed or naked as we find the only orientation we have or need is the one whereby we keep in touch with God. We constantly thank him for his gifts and grace in a prayerful embrace where Divine and human spirits become one. But there is no need for this approach to be restricted to those who live in religious houses. The attraction of the Rule of Benedict is that when we use it with informed interpretation, we find it becomes a guide to the way of life that leads us to God and keeps us there.

Jesus once told a parable about a rich man whose land provides him with a very good income. The harvest is so good, in fact, that the man has no room to store all his grain and goods. So he decides to pull down his existing barns and build bigger ones. Then he can relax, eat, drink and be merry. 'Nothing much wrong with that,' we might think, as good capitalists. The man is clearly very good at what he does and is fortunate in the degree of his financial security. Thus far, it is a familiar story told all over the capitalist world. Yet in the parable, Jesus does not describe this man as blessed. Far from it. Instead, Jesus says that God addresses the man as a fool saying, 'This very night your life is being demanded of you. And the things you have prepared, whose will they be?' Jesus concludes the story by saying, 'So it is with those who store up treasures for themselves but are not rich towards God.'[9] We can understand from this and other stories and sayings of Jesus that what is most important to God is not how long we live, how much money we earn or how many possessions we have. What matters most is the condition of our souls. Unsurprisingly in a materialistic society, this is a highly unfashionable message to promote today. In a society where we place such great importance on material possessions, we can quickly forget that what matters most is our spiritual progress towards God. Come to think of it, what fool puts his trust in material matters today where stock-market crash, unanticipated ill-health or even what we refer to as an 'act of God' can reduce us to so much ash in an instant?

In his final chapter, Benedict writes:

Are you hastening toward your heavenly home? Then with Christ's help, keep this little rule that we have written for beginners. After that you can set out for the loftier summits of the teaching and virtues we mentioned above, and under God's protection you will reach them. (RB 73.8–9)

His question is clearly rhetorical. He expects us to understand the aim of our lives in terms of hastening towards our heavenly home. But we would not usually describe how we live in such terms. Our first reaction might be to think that such an exhortation falls into the category of the unnecessarily morbid. Yet Benedict is not trying to encourage us to wish our life away. He is pointing out to us where our priorities should lie. For to live as if your priority is to keep in touch with God by enjoying his love in this world and the next, is to turn upside down the natural priorities we assume in life.

I suspect we shall be very surprised sometime soon when the full extent of our genetic conditioning and innate instinctual behaviour is revealed. We may feel now, if not at some time in the future, that we are not as free-thinking in our behaviour or in the choices we make in life as we suppose. A very considerable amount of our human behaviour is conditioned by culture or inheritance and also genetic disposition, from hereditary illnesses to a predisposition to destructive patterns of behaviour. The moralists and fundamentalists have been quick to deplore and condemn those whose human nature has contained what they consider to be aberrant behaviour. Their reaction has been to resort to an outdated theistic understanding of God, where salvation is sought through self-condemnation as much as anything. Most of us, thankfully, are far more enlightened than this. We realize that salvation is to be understood today as the process of coming to terms with oneself in a way by which we come to terms with God. Otherwise, you end up condemning people for being created as they are. Such concepts of original sin are more than unhelpful. They deny the incarnation of a God of love who in Jesus Christ welcomes the outcast, misfit and marginalized and rejects those who think they are somehow better, more religious, people than others.

So we search for a spirituality by which we can recognize and encourage the helpful desires and passions with which we are born. At the same time we aim to overcome the unhelpful ones. They were once important tools for survival in an evolving world but today threaten our future. We find the Way to do this through Jesus of Nazareth, who by the nature of his Divine love in human being, was recognized as the Christ not only of the Church but also of the universe.[10] And as we attempt to follow this Way, we seek to blend the wisdom and prayers of those who have gone before us with our understanding of our faith today. The Rule of St Benedict, who himself was not afraid to use the ideas of others, gives us an effective means to achieve this kind of synthesis by which we can come to experience and enjoy the love that keeps us in touch with ourselves and our loved ones, and with God.

As we open our hearts increasingly to this love of God, we are likely from time to time to echo the words of the father of the sick child who said to Jesus, 'I believe you, help me to believe you more'.[11] Our nascent belief may at this stage be no more developed than a strong inkling that God is out there somewhere and we may doubt that we are knowledgeable enough. But if belief is understood principally in terms of knowledge – in the sense that the more one knows, the more faith one can have – we can be seriously misled. For in many ways, the more knowledge one has, the harder it is to be faithful. It is more helpful instead to say, 'I love you, help me to love you more.' For love is about commitment, and the more commitment we have, the more faith we shall have. Then as we commit ourselves to love and nothing else, we begin to see glimpses of a Divine purpose in our lives. And in our emerging love, we discover God's 'yes' to ourselves and a future hitherto unexpected and unexplored.

\* \* \*

## *From the Rule of St Benedict*

But for anyone hastening on to the perfection of monastic life, there are the teachings of the holy Fathers, the observance of which will lead him to the very heights of perfection. What page, what passage of the inspired books of the Old and New Testaments is not the truest of guides for human life? What book of the holy catholic Fathers does not resoundingly summon us along the true way to reach the Creator. (RB 73.3–4)

## *For reflection*

A brother came to a hermit: and as he was taking his leave, he said, 'Forgive me, abba, for preventing you from keeping your rule.' The hermit answered, 'My rule is to welcome you with hospitality, and to send you on your way in peace.'[12]

### Something to do

Work out a Rule of Life which will help you to keep in touch with all that is important to you. (You may like to adopt a Benedictine way of doing this.[13]) This may include the following:

- Decide on a regular pattern of prayer both individual and corporate.
- Set a time aside for Bible or spiritual reading on a regular basis, according to the pattern of *lectio divina*.
- Form a regular pattern of Bible study and wider spiritual reading and reflection.
- Work out how best to use your resources responsibly to help yourself and your loved ones and also those in need.
- Share your Rule with friends to make sure you have set yourself achievable goals. Better still, find someone who will either adopt a similar Rule of Life with you or who will act as a mentor or spiritual guide for you, helping you at regular intervals to reflect on how you are getting on.

- Offer yourself and your commitment to live out the Rule to God.

## A Bible passage to consider

Then he said to Thomas, 'Put your finger here and see my hands. Reach out your hand and put it in my side. Do not doubt but believe.' (John 20.27)

## Prayer

Christ of the universe
where love and pain coincide
in heartfelt communion
may we praise
and serve you for ever
in life and in death.
Amen.

# Notes

## Introduction

1 Eva Heymann, *The Deep Centre* (Darton, Longman and Todd, 2006), p. 10.

## 1 The desire to hide

1 The *Sayings of the Fathers* were one of the principal sources used by St Benedict in drawing up his Rule and in his appreciation of the spiritual life.
2 *The Desert Fathers: The Sayings of the Early Christian Monks*, trans. Benedicta Ward (Penguin Books, 2003), p. 118.
3 Joan Chittister OSB, *Wisdom Distilled from the Daily: Living the Rule of St Benedict Today* (HarperCollins, 1991), p. 111.
4 Timothy Radcliffe OP, *Seven Last Words* (Burns and Oates, 2004), p. 52.
5 Luke 9.58.
6 Romans 13.11.
7 See Psalm 95.7–8.

## 2 The love of God

1 John 3.16–17.
2 Quoted by John O'Donohue in *Anam Cara* (Bantam Books, 1999), p. 46.
3 St Augustine lived from AD 354 to 430.
4 St Augustine, *Confessions*, trans. and ed. R. S. Pine-Coffin (Penguin, 1961), Book 4 Chapter 2, p. 92.
5 Matthew 5.8.
6 Mark 12.30–31.
7 Augustine, *Confessions*, Book 13 Chapter 2, p. 131.
8 *The Desert Fathers: The Sayings of the Early Christian Monks*, trans. Benedicta Ward (Penguin Books, 2003), p. 143.

## 3 The desire to fulfil the dreams of others

1 See Mark 12.18–31.
2 See David Mearns and Brian Thorne, *Person-Centred Counselling in Action* (Sage Publications, 1995, first published 1988), pp. 10ff.
3 Luke 17.21 (NIV).
4 See Matthew 7.1: 'Do not judge, so that you may not be judged.'

## 4 The love of simplicity

1 This saying is attributed to Evagrius who was one of the academics of fourth-century monasticism. *The Desert Fathers: The Sayings of the Early Christian Monks*, trans. Benedicta Ward (Penguin Books, 2003), p. 10.
2 Father Evgraf Kovalevsky, quoted by Metropolitan Anthony of Sourozh, *Encounter* (Darton, Longman and Todd, 2005), p. 267.
3 Psalm 42.7.
4 John O'Donohue, *Anam Cara* (Bantam Books, 1999), p. 51.
5 Darkness, to the Hebrew mind, of course symbolized a meaningless chaos that threatened to overcome the order that was needed to create and sustain life. Hence in the first creation story we read that the first words God said over a world in darkness and chaos were, 'Let there be light.' And now, here among human beings, is that very Light, in the person of Jesus.

## 5 The desire for erotic love

1 See Jo Ind, *Memories of Bliss: God, Sex, and Us* (SCM Press, 2003), pp. 73ff.
2 John 4.1–42.
3 This is not the same as the story where people ask a question concerning remarriage to try and catch Jesus out. In a culture where, if a woman's husband died it was the tradition that his closest living male relative, usually his brother, would take the widow as his wife and responsibility, these people want to know which husband a woman will have in heaven if, following this tradition, she ends up with seven husbands on earth (Matt. 22.23–28). Nor is it the same as the story of the woman caught in the very act of adultery (John 8.1–11).
4 Anthony de Mello, *One Minute Wisdom* (an Image Book, published by Doubleday, 1985), p. 120.

## 6 The love of wholeness

1 Mark 8.35–36.
2 St Maximus the Confessor; see Dumitru Staniloe, trans. Archimandrite Jerome (Newville) and Otilia Kloos, *Orthodox Spirituality* (St Tikhon's Seminary Press, 2002), p. 91.
3 St Maximus the Confessor, Staniloe, *Orthodox Spirituality*, p. 85.
4 1 John 4.16.
5 From The Solemnization of Matrimony in The Book of Common Prayer.
6 From The Marriage Service, *Common Worship: Pastoral Services* (Church House Publishing, 2000; copyright ©The Archbishops' Council, 2000).
7 Song of Solomon 8.6–7.
8 *The Desert Fathers: The Sayings of the Early Christian Monks*, trans. Benedicta Ward (Penguin Books, 2003), p. 132.

## 7 The desire for hatred

1 This extract is taken from *Les Misérables* by Alain Boublil and Claude Michel Schönberg, English lyrics by Herbert Kretzmer. With kind permission of Alain Boublil Overseas Limited.
2 Matthew 5.44.
3 John 8.32.
4 Laura Swan OSB, *The Forgotten Desert Mothers* (Paulist Press, 2001), p. 5.
5 See Oliver McTernan, *Violence in God's Name* (Darton, Longman and Todd, 2003), pp. 45–76.
6 Luke 14.25–33.
7 See the Parable of the Talents, Matthew 25.14–30.
8 Swan, *Forgotten Desert Mothers*, p. 61.
9 Aquinata Böckmann OSB, *Perspectives on the Rule of St Benedict* (The Liturgical Press, 2005), p. 181.

## 8 The love of forgiveness

1 See Matthew 10.8 (NIV).
2 Hebrews 13.2.
3 *The Desert Fathers: The Sayings of the Early Christian Monks*, trans. Benedicta Ward (Penguin Books, 2003), p. 177.
4 Matthew 22.36–40.

5 Matthew 5.21–25.

6 Genesis 4.

7 *The Desert Fathers*, p. 85.

8 RB Prologue 49.

9 Mark 11.25.

10 Mark 9.24.

11 Dietrich Bonhoeffer, *The Cost of Discipleship* (SCM Press, 1959, first published 1948), pp. 36–7.

12 *The Desert Fathers*, p. 23.

## 9 The desire to be in control

1 Mark 10.22.

2 Matthew 21.33–42.

3 Genesis 2.15—3.24.

4 Genesis 2.7.

5 Matthew 1.23.

6 Andrew Clitherow, *Renewing Faith in Ordained Ministry* (SPCK, 2004), p. 45.

7 St John of the Ladder, *The Ladder of Divine Ascent* Step 23; see Father John Mack, *Ascending the Heights* (Conciliar Press, 1999), p. 117.

8 *The Desert Fathers: The Sayings of the Early Christian Monks*, trans. Benedicta Ward (Penguin Books, 2003), p. 119.

## 10 The love of letting go

1 I am indebted to Canon Dick Cartmell (whose restless prophetic voice has disturbed the comfortable Christian assumptions of many), his wife Hiddy, and the people of the parish of St James, Lower Darwen, for working with me and the people of St Paul's Scotforth, to set this up as a joint project some years ago.

2 Psalm 51.15, referred to in this instance in Morning Prayer in *Common Worship: Daily Prayer* (Church House Publishing, 2005; copyright © The Archbishops' Council, 2005).

3 On 1 January 2008, more than 30 women and children were burned to death in an Assemblies of God church in Eldoret, in the west of Kenya. The dead were Kikuyu, the same ethnic group as the recently re-elected president, Mwai Kibaki, and had taken refuge for fear of being attacked by supporters of the President's rival, Raila Odinga, who had accused Kibaki of election fraud.

4 See Barbara Glasson, *I am Somewhere Else* (Darton, Longman and Todd, 2006).
5 John 3.8.
6 Sara Maitland, *A Big-Enough God* (Mowbray, 1995), p. 267.
7 Father Evgraf Kovalevsky, quoted by Metropolitan Anthony of Sourozh in *Encounter* (Darton, Longman and Todd, 2005), p. 267.
8 Mark 1.35–39.
9 *The Desert Fathers: The Sayings of the Early Christian Monks*, trans. Benedicta Ward (Penguin Books, 2003), p. 158.

## 11 The desire to live for ever

1 Mary and Ellen Lukas, *Teilhard* (William Collins and Sons, 1977), p. 23.
2 P. Teilhard de Chardin, *Hymn of the Universe* (William Collins and Sons, 1965), 'The Mass on the World', p. 28.
3 P. Teilhard de Chardin, *Christianity and Evolution* (Harvest/Harcourt, 1974), p. 163.
4 Teilhard de Chardin, *Christianity and Evolution*, p. 219.
5 P. Teilhard de Chardin, *The Phenomenon of Man* (Perennial/HarperCollins, 2002), p. 251.
6 See Matthew 12.30; 6.24; John 12.25.
7 John 3.16.
8 St Anthony is thought to have lived from AD 251 to 336.
9 St Augustine, *Confessions*, trans. R. S. Pine-Coffin (Penguin Books, 1961), p. 115.
10 St Augustine, *City of God*, trans Henry Bettenson, ed. David Knowles (Penguin Books, 1972), p. 1028.
11 *The Desert Fathers: The Sayings of the Early Christian Monks*, trans. Benedicta Ward (Penguin Books, 2003), p. 89.
12 1 Peter 4.1–2.
13 Galatians 2.20.
14 Mark 13.32.
15 Mark 15.34.
16 Mark 9.49–50.
17 See Michael Mayne, *The Enduring Melody* (Darton, Longman and Todd, 2006), p. 207.
18 Ephesians 3.18–19.
19 John 14.6.

20 Teilhard de Chardin, *Hymn of the Universe*, p. 32, where Teilhard notes that the word 'ego' refers to 'the proud, defiant self-reliance, the attempted autonomy, of man in revolt against God'.

## 12 The love that keeps you in touch

1 Acts 17.28.
2 *Athanasius: The Life of Antony and The Letter to Marcellinus*, trans. Robert Gregg (Paulist Press, 1980), p. 97.
3 Esther de Waal, *Seeking God* (Canterbury Press, 1999), p. 93.
4 Benedict encouraged spiritual reading, particularly in Lent (RB 48.14–16).
5 The Fathers of the early Church were theologians and spiritual giants principally of the first five centuries.
6 A most helpful introduction to this is David Foster OSB, *Reading with God: lectio divina* (Continuum, 2005).
7 Throughout this book, there have been constant references to the Desert Fathers and I hope that this will encourage the reader to read the writings of the Early Fathers or to discover this rich vein of spirituality.
8 For those who want to know more about this and practise it in their daily lives, there are suggestions in the 'Further reading' section.
9 Luke 12.16–21.
10 Colossians 1.15–20.
11 Mark 9.24 (paraphrased).
12 *The Desert Fathers: The Sayings of the Early Christian Monks*, trans. Benedicta Ward (Penguin Books, 2003), p. 136.
13 You may find some of the suggestions in the 'Further reading' section helpful.

# Further reading

Joan Chittister OSB, *Wisdom Distilled from the Daily: Living the Rule of St Benedict* (HarperCollins, 1991).

A. Marett Crosby, *The Benedictine Handbook* (Canterbury Press, 2003).

Will Derks, *The Rule of Benedict for Beginners: Spirituality for Daily Life* (The Liturgical Press, 2003).

David Foster OSB, *Reading with God: lectio divina* (Continuum, 2005).

Maxwell E. Johnson (compiler and editor), *Benedictine Daily Prayer: A Short Breviary* (Columba Press, 2005).

Christopher Jamieson, Abbot of Worth, *Finding Sanctuary* (Weidenfeld and Nicholson, 2006).

Terence G. Kardong, *Day by Day with Saint Benedict* (The Liturgical Press, 2005).

Dwight Longenecker, *Listen, My Son: St Benedict for Fathers* (Gracewing, 2000).

John McQuistan, *Always We Begin Again: The Benedictine Way* (Continuum, 1991).

Kathleen Norris, Patrick Barry and Richard Yeo, *Wisdom from the Monastery* (Canterbury Press, 2005).

Diarmuid O'Murchu, *The Transformation of Desire* (Darton, Longman and Todd, 2007).

Abbot Parry OSB and Esther de Waal, *The Rule of St Benedict* (Gracewing Fowler Wright Books, 1990).

*St Benedict's Prayer Book* (Ampleforth Abbey Press, 1993).

Philip Sheldrake, *Befriending our Desires* (Novalis and Darton, Longman and Todd, 2001).

Brian C. Taylor, *Spirituality for Everyday Living: An Adaptation of the Rule of St Benedict* (The Liturgical Press, 1999).

Jane Tomaine, *St Benedict's Toolbox: The Nuts and Bolts of Everyday Benedictine Living* (Continuum, 2005).

Korneel Vermeiren OCSO, *Praying with Benedict* (Darton, Longman and Todd, 1999).

Esther de Waal, *Seeking God: The Way of St Benedict* (Canterbury Press, 1984).

Esther de Waal, *Living with Contradiction: An Introduction to Benedictine Spirituality* (Canterbury Press, 1989).

Esther de Waal, *A Life-Giving Way: A Commentary on the Rule on St Benedict* (Mowbray, 1995).